T0265898

Advance Praise

"Here is a book that speaks comprehensively and powerfully to the unique challenge of running a foundation. With practical insights and wisdom gleaned from years of experience, Malcolm Macleod explores the crucial elements required for impact, from building strong relationships with nonprofits to getting the most out of a governing board to managing an endowment. Skillfully weaving powerful stories of impact that remind us why this work matters with practical insights and tips for those who find themselves leading foundations, Macleod's book is the most comprehensive resource for foundation leaders I have seen. Every foundation CEO, aspiring CEO, and board member needs this book."

—PHIL BUCHANAN, president, Center for Effective Philanthropy, and author of *Giving Done Right: Effective Philanthropy and Making Every Dollar Count*

"*The Practice of Philanthropy* is a readable guide to grantmaking, investing, and the business of running a foundation. It combines practical advice from Malcolm's many years of doing this work with his deep knowledge of the principles behind it. This book is full of advice and examples that foundation leaders will either recognize or face in the future. It will help foundation leaders achieve impact and the satisfaction that comes with it."

—The Right Honourable PAUL MARTIN, Canada's twenty-first prime minister

"If you are looking for a practical guide to running a foundation, look no further. Malcolm Macleod draws on his diverse experience as both a foundation staff person and a foundation board member to share truly useful advice on grantmaking, governance, and investing. This book is an excellent resource for anyone working in the foundation space and in particular for small- and medium-sized foundations."

—KIRSTEN ROUSE, executive director, Fundy Community Foundation

"*The Practice of Philanthropy* is an indispensable resource for everyone involved in the world of grantmaking foundations. Drawing on his years of experience as past president and CEO of the Johnson Scholarship Foundation and his career as a lawyer, Malcolm Macleod has written a book that offers clear, concise, wise, and insightful guidance on a range of key topics. There is no other book quite like it in Canada or the United States."

—PROFESSOR DAVID BLAIKIE, Schulich School of Law, Dalhousie University, and Bora Laskin Faculty of Law, Lakehead University (retired)

"Malcolm's title, *The Practice of Philanthropy*, could not be more apt. This is an invaluable 'how-to' guide based on three decades of experience. He shares many of the dos and don'ts of leading a nonprofit organization. But the word 'practice' also invokes that taking the best lessons from business can lead to a more effective foundation. Do some of the rules that define a well-run law practice or investment management partnership apply to small nonprofits? This book paints that picture—how to tackle the challenge of doing the greatest good with the limited funds and human capital that every foundation has at its disposal. Malcolm sees his investments in grantee 'partners' in terms of maximizing return on investment, leveraging investments where possible, taking calculated risks to find new solutions, and on how working with the 'customer' collaboratively leads to a better understanding of the grantee's true needs."

—MIKE MILLER, JSF board member and former head of global equities, BMO Capital Markets

"I applaud Malcolm for sharing his voice and expertise on how philanthropy can authentically create systems of equity and inclusion for underserved communities. His insights on investing in Native communities for nearly thirty years is an example to be commended and replicated. He understands that investing in diversity is not just a financial commitment but one that empowers leaders in and of the communities you are committed to serving. Board leadership, consultants, and long-term relationships are key to genuine partnerships and impacts. I encourage anyone looking to take equity to the next level to get this book!"

—ANGELIQUE ALBERT, CEO, Native Forward Scholars Fund,
citizen of Confederated Salish and Kootenai Tribes

"Malcolm's leadership skills, insight, and knowledge of philanthropy have been essential to the growth and development of the Johnson Scholarship Foundation. In his leadership roles at JSF, he has successfully guided the organization by keeping the mission in mind at all times while skillfully overseeing grantmaking, endowment investing, and staff and board development. He has a deep understanding of what goes into effective grantmaking, and as a former grantee I can attest first-hand to his exceptional abilities in developing and maintaining effective and fruitful relationships with grantee organizations. Malcolm's understanding of governance processes and effective board engagement and development practices is also exceptional. As a leader and as an adviser to foundations, his skill set is comprehensive and deep. His years of experience, coupled with his excellent insight and tremendous analytical skills, make him a tremendous resource for foundations seeking to become more effective in achieving their mission."

—BILL CORWIN, president, Mission Velocity

"I can recommend this as a guide to giving for those who care and have been blessed as stewards of donated resources for the greater good of intended recipients."

—DAVID HAYWARD, president, New Brunswick Children's Foundation

MALCOLM MACLEOD

The Practice of
Philanthropy

A GUIDE FOR
FOUNDATION BOARDS
AND STAFF

BARLOW
BOOKS

Main text copyright © Malcolm Macleod, 2023
Foreword copyright © The Right Honourable Paul Martin, 2023

ISBN 978-1-998841-02-8 (hardcover)
ISBN 978-1-998841-05-9 (ebook)

Printed in Canada

Publisher: Sarah Scott
Book producer: Tracy Bordian/At Large Editorial Services
Cover design: Paul Hodgson
Interior design and layout: Ruth Dwight
Developmental editor: Eleanor Gasparik
Copy editor: Dawn Hunter

For more information, visit www.barlowbooks.com

Barlow Book Publishing Inc.
96 Elm Avenue, Toronto, ON
M4W 1P2 Canada

BARLOW
BOOKS

For Barbara,
my love and my hero

Contents

Foreword

When I began to build The Martin Family Initiative, I soon realized that there was more to making and executing philanthropic grants than I had imagined. My experience in business and government was helpful, but it did not prepare me for the unique challenges of running a family foundation. Philanthropy demands its own set of skills and knowledge, and I had to learn on the job. I needed guidance, and that was when I turned to Malcolm Macleod.

I met Malcolm when I left government. He was the president of the Johnson Scholarship Foundation, a private foundation based in the United States that made grants in the United States and Canada. I was impressed by Malcolm's approach to philanthropy, and we became good friends and partners in the pursuit of our respective missions. Malcolm had been doing this for a number of years by this time, and I sought his help and advice on how to best fulfill the potential of my foundation. Our discussions were both theoretical and practical, and most importantly, Malcolm's advice has been invaluable in helping me do what had to be done.

The Johnson Scholarship Foundation is clearly a model to follow. It has a stellar board and a lean, efficient staff. Its members are drawn from all walks of life and each one brings a particular expertise to the work of the foundation. I have been to several foundation meetings, and I am always struck by their collegiality and sense of purpose. It was apparent to me that Malcolm, as leader of this foundation, had been able to translate his ideas on philanthropy and foundations into action.

When Malcolm retired as president of the foundation in 2020, I urged him to write a book about philanthropy and foundations. There is a tremendous need for such a book, and he is uniquely qualified to write it. In his prior life he was a successful lawyer, and he brings impressive analytical and communication skills to bear on the practice of philanthropy. His thirty years as a foundation leader give him an authoritative perspective. In addition to reading, writing, and talking about philanthropy, he has actually practiced it. He led the board, staff, and consultants who invested the foundation's endowment and made its grants.

The Practice of Philanthropy is a readable guide to grantmaking, investing, and the business of running a foundation. It combines practical advice from Malcolm's many years of doing this work with his deep knowledge of the principles behind it. This book is full of advice and examples that foundation leaders will either recognize or face in the future. It takes you inside a grantmaking foundation and gives a feel for its basic operations and, importantly, the practical steps to execute them well. This book will help foundation leaders achieve impact and the satisfaction that comes with it.

We are amid one of the largest generational transfers of wealth in history. There are over one hundred thousand foundations in North America with assets of over $1.5 trillion. The number of foundations and their assets will continue to increase for the foreseeable future. These foundations enjoy a unique freedom in our society. Their sole purpose is to make the world a better place and they can make whatever grants they think will best accomplish this. They are not beholden to shareholders or an electorate. They are free to experiment, to risk failure, and to take a long view in their grantmaking. This is the stuff of change and innovation that neither government nor business has.

Foundations are essential to social progress and tools such as this book will help them to do a better job and be more effective. I recommend *The Practice of Philanthropy* to you. It will help you to realize your potential as a foundation leader and make a positive difference in society, and you will enjoy yourself in the process.

Paul Martin

The Right Honourable Paul Martin bought Canada Steamship Lines in 1981 and later served in government as minister of finance and then as Canada's twenty-first prime minister. The Kelowna Accord was one of his notable achievements as prime minister and, after leaving government, he founded The Martin Family Initiative to pursue a lifelong passion: the advancement of Indigenous Peoples in Canada.

Introduction

If you are a board member or staff of a grantmaking foundation, I have written this book for you. My hope is to give you, a foundation leader, a better feel for the practice of philanthropy and to help you make more impactful grants, achieve sustainable investment returns, and build better boards. This book does not deal with tax planning or the legal aspects of establishing a foundation. Nor is it about fundraising. This book covers subjects that have not received enough attention. What does good grantmaking look like? What should it try to accomplish? What are the steps to good grantmaking? What is the role of foundation leaders in financial investing? How do they create and maintain healthy, useful boards? These are the substantive issues of foundation practice, and foundation leaders must understand them for their foundations to succeed.

This is a book for all types of grantmaking foundations, American and Canadian, community and private. There are legal and technical differences among types of foundations but the essentials of grant-making, investing, and board and staff service are universal.

Andrew Carnegie wrote that 95 percent of philanthropy is wasted and actually contributes to the very ills that it seeks to redress. This is as true today as it was one hundred years ago. The problem is insufficient thought, investigation, and analysis by grantmakers. Later in this book, I discuss foundation performance in detail, but for now I will use an example that we can all relate to. Many of us will happily spend hours researching the purchase of a new television but little time researching for charitable contributions. If we thought about it, we would realize that giving money without investigation or analysis is unlikely to yield productive results. This issue is even more relevant for foundations. Grantmaking is their business, their reason for being. Grants are the investments that foundations make to catalyze social change. Foundations that sidestep the rigors of strategy, knowledge, thought and energy do not solve problems. They simply perpetuate dependance upon more grants.

Grantmaking foundations vary greatly in mission, management style, and complexity. There is a lighthearted saying in our industry: "If you have seen one private foundation then . . . you have seen one private foundation." Each one is unique. Because foundations are not common to the everyday experience of most people, their operations are not well understood. Foundations have two essential operations: investing their endowment and making grants. Grantmaking is the more difficult, but both are equally important. Investment returns are the fuel for foundation grantmaking.

People, especially those outside philanthropy, tend to evaluate foundations according to the size of their endowments. This is hardly surprising, especially in an industry that has few objective measures.

However, it is misguided to judge a foundation by the amount of money it has. What is its mission? What does it do? How does it do it? What are the results of its investing and grantmaking? These questions are difficult, if not impossible, for outsiders to answer but would tell us much more about a foundation's value. It should come as no surprise that a foundation's quality does not always correlate to the size of its endowment. Many smaller foundations have stellar boards and are better investors and grantmakers than their larger counterparts.

NORTH AMERICA'S FOUNDATION UNIVERSE

There are about 130,000 private and community foundations in the United States[1] and 6,000 in Canada.[2] Collectively they have assets of about $1.5 trillion and make annual grants of almost $85 billion.[3] Only 150 foundations have assets of $1 billion or more. These are the giants of the foundation universe. The biggest of these is the Bill & Melinda Gates Foundation, which has an endowment of $51 billion. There are about 1,200 large foundations with assets between $100 million and $1 billion.

The rest of the foundations, over 99 percent, have assets from a few thousand dollars to $100 million. Collectively, these foundations have more money than either the giants or the large foundations. They make most of the grants and comprise the overwhelming majority of the people.[4] Their philanthropic impact is much bigger than most of them realize.

If we reject size as a measure and accept our inability to objectively rank foundations according to the quality of their operations, we still need a way to easily categorize them and make sense of the foundation universe. Exponent Philanthropy, formerly the Association of Small Foundations, describes its membership as funders that practice philanthropy with few or no staff. The number of staff is a more useful descriptor than the size of its endowment. "Few or no staff" usually tells us that the board is directly engaged in the supervision or performance of grantmaking and investment tasks, regardless of how much money the foundation has.

If you are part of a grantmaking foundation with few or no staff and you aspire to improve foundation performance and impact, then I had you in mind when I wrote this book.

Most of us come to foundation leadership with no prior training or experience. We must learn as we go along, which is not ideal. The arts of good foundation practice are not readily apparent, and much of what leaders need to know is counterintuitive. Learning from peers is also difficult, not because they are unwilling to share but because foundations are notoriously idiosyncratic and have few standardized procedures and precedents. In the absence of accessible training, foundation leaders must grope their way along by trial and error and learn as lessons present themselves. This is what I did, and it took far too long. I constantly thought, *There has to be a better way.*

This book provides insight and information that would otherwise take years to acquire and will serve as a reference for your foundation practice. It shows the difference between cavalier grantmaking and grantmaking that achieves lasting impact, and it outlines the essential steps to achieve the latter. It explains the importance of foundation values, vision, mission, and strategy and how each can be developed.

It examines principles of investment management that will help your foundation achieve sustainable financial investment returns. It explains how good foundation leaders build resilient and productive organizations by recruiting and engaging a board, working with staff (for foundations that have staff), and nurturing foundation culture by transparent governance and other healthy practices. This book discusses eleven grants made by our foundation, some successful and others not. The stories will help foundation leaders avoid our mistakes and share with them the exhilaration that comes from grants that achieved impact. This is the reference book I needed at the beginning of my run as a foundation leader.

In this book I take you on my journey as a board member and president of the Johnson Scholarship Foundation (JSF), a private foundation with a mission to assist people with financial need to obtain education and employment. We began with a single employee and now operate with a staff of four. JSF has an engaged board that sets grantmaking priorities and strategy, interacts with grantees, and reviews and decides each grant application. I tell you what we learned and how, what worked, what I was afraid of, and the mistakes I made. I bring you inside and give you an understanding of what foundation work is and how it can be practiced. The lessons and principles in this book are applicable to all foundations with few or no staff that aspire to make a difference, regardless of whether they work in a boardroom or around a kitchen table.

In my prior life, I was a partner in a large law firm. I thought of myself as a quick study and, when I was appointed president of JSF, I was the picture of confidence. I was well acquainted with boardrooms and had prior experience on the foundation's investment committee. As for grantmaking, I reasoned that since we already had the money, giving it away should not be difficult. However, when I came face to face with my lack of skills and knowledge to do the work, I realized that I was completely out of my element. I soon understood it is easy to distribute money, but difficult to make grants that catalyze change. I felt like an imposter! What would I do?

In his book *Outliers*,[5] Malcolm Gladwell posits that it takes ten thousand hours of practice to learn one's craft. That is my experience. My education as a grantmaker has come from dealing with and listening to grantees, researchers, authors, teachers, and peers. Important insights come to me when I least expect them and often from seemingly unlikely sources. I started by going to conferences. They did not offer much continuing professional education, but I was often invigorated and enlightened by a speaker. At a Council on Foundations conference, Ron Chernow spoke about his new book, *Titan: The Life of John D. Rockefeller, Sr.*[6] Its account of Rockefeller's philanthropy is both personal and analytical and is one of the best books on grantmaking that I have ever read.

I took a course for philanthropic leaders at Stanford University, which changed the way that I thought about foundation grantees. I spent a day talking with an Indigenous lawyer on the Pine Ridge Reservation, and this conversation is still my framework for grantmaking in service of Indigenous Peoples. Most of what I have learned has come from grantees, potential grantees, and the people that they serve.

My plight is typical of all newcomers, whether they know it or not. I have seen many foundations, big and small, start with great confidence and expectations. They are often led by people who have excelled in business and have a knack for getting things done quickly and efficiently. They assume that they will be able to do the same thing in their foundation but soon realize that it is more complicated than that. It takes time to learn this business, regardless of your foundation's size or your expertise in other work.

I was fortunate to have patient mentors and a tolerant board that wanted me to succeed. I had the time to learn and get better. I also needed time to come to terms with the emotional aspects of investing and grantmaking, particularly grantmaking. If grantmaking is supposed to catalyze change, why can't we seem to do that? What are we missing? It took time to realize that, although the opportunity is special, there is nothing special about the work or the people doing it. Perfection and supernatural wisdom are unhelpful illusions.

The board and I continued to accumulate experience and knowledge about the foundation's fields of interest. Our board recruiting efforts targeted people who had special knowledge in our fields of interest, and we began to regularly evaluate the level of contribution and interest of sitting board members. Foundation performance improved. The grant committee shaped strategies, and grantmaking became more impactful. We began to gain confidence in our work and to take on more risk. On the investment front, JSF's investment returns since 1995 are in the top quartile among its peers.[7] JSF is better than it was twenty years ago, and it tries to improve every year.

Leading a foundation is a practice. The practice varies greatly from one foundation to another, and what works well for one may not work for another. This is not to say anything goes. There are principles that underlie effective foundation practice. To become proficient, foundation leaders need to understand, apply, and adapt them to their foundation. This book explains these principles and shows what effective foundation practice looks like. New foundation leaders will better understand philanthropy, and the more experienced will add to their knowledge. In both cases, the ability to practice philanthropy will improve, and future lessons will be easier to recognize and absorb.

Although this book will shorten your learning curve, it does not provide easy ways to make effective grants or achieve high investment returns. Excellent foundation practice is hard work and requires rigorous discipline and effort, thought, energy, gumption, and risk taking. Foundation leaders have been given a unique opportunity, one that most people do not get. They have been given the freedom to invest money in other people and organizations to help make society better. They must choose how they will use that opportunity. Will they undertake the rigors of excellent foundation practice, or will they go through the motions?

Successful foundation leaders are defined by the choice that they make and not the opportunity they have been given, the amount of money at their disposal, or even their talent. If you choose to learn and apply the basic principles of philanthropic practice and wholeheartedly throw yourself into this work, then success will surely follow. Your foundation will flourish and its grantmaking will achieve impact. The nonmonetary rewards of impactful grantmaking are thrilling. The changes that your foundation's grants help bring about and your relationships with the people doing the work will greatly surpass your expectations and give you long-lasting satisfaction.

1

The Essence of Grantmaking

As the title suggests, this chapter delves into the essential elements of grantmaking. It discusses some of the unique challenges faced by grantmakers, foundation performance in the face of these challenges, and approaches that have produced effective grantmaking. It also offers the conceptual framework of grants as investments, which will assist the practicing grantmaker. The next chapter—Seven Stories and Ten Principles—brings this discussion to life and illustrates what grantmaking looks like, both good and bad. It ends with ten principles that underpin good grantmaking.

The good news is that the fundamentals of good grantmaking can be easily understood and practiced by foundations of any type, style, and size.

GOOD GRANTMAKING IS DIFFICULT BECAUSE IT SEEKS FINALITIES

Grantmaking is more than just handing out money. The goal of good grantmaking is to make a difference, to improve society. John D. Rockefeller and Andrew Carnegie—titans of both business and philanthropy—each said that their money was easier to make than to give away. What they meant is to give money away effectively, to make a positive difference in the world, is more difficult than making money. Peter Frumkin sums it up well in the preface of his excellent treatise, *The Essence of Strategic Giving*:

> Much of philanthropy is directed at addressing human problems that are multifaceted, do not have single solutions, and are often shaped by a huge range of factors that lie outside the span of control of the donor or the organization delivering the actual charitable service. In this context of causal uncertainty and ambiguity, donors would appear to have their work cut out for them.[8]

Consider the grantmaking journey of John D. Rockefeller. In his time, or perhaps any time, he was the richest person in the world. His net worth was today's equivalent of $280 billion, over three times the Gates' fortune.[9] Rockefeller's astounding wealth and hard-driving business practices brought him a reputation for avarice. The story of how Rockefeller had swindled "the widow Backus" out of her late husband's oil business was widely reported and it fueled populist outrage. The story was bogus, but it nevertheless stuck and made its way into the world's folklore for generations, a morality tale of unbridled capitalism run amok.[10]

Rockefeller was a religious man and believed that his great wealth was ordained and that God had chosen him to accumulate a fortune so that he could use it to do good. He thought that he was God's trustee. One can easily imagine the pressure on him. He felt misunderstood and unfairly reviled, was dogged by the press, and saw himself as accountable to God. He lamented in 1899, ten years into his philanthropic career:

> About the year 1890 I was still following the haphazard fashion of giving here and there as appeals presented themselves. I investigated as I could, and worked myself almost to a nervous breakdown in groping my way, without sufficient guide or chart, through an ever-widening field of philanthropic endeavor. It was forced upon me to organize and plan this department upon as distinct lines of progress as our other business affairs.[11]

Rockefeller's reference to "a nervous breakdown" is no exaggeration. His angst was at times incapacitating.[12] He could have made large gifts to established charities and causes. This would have dispensed his wealth more quickly and solved his public relations problem. But Rockefeller was not playing to the gallery. He had thought deeply and knew that it wasn't enough just to give his money away.

Rockefeller was determined not to make grants that continued or created dependence: "The best philanthropy," he wrote, "is constantly in search of finalities—a search for a cause, an attempt to cure evils at their source."[13] Rockefeller's high standards for grantmaking contributed to his anxiety, but he persevered and became one of history's great philanthropists. Grantmakers of all sizes can take heart from Rockefeller's experience. If you are confused about what to do or how to do it, that is a good start. You are in good company.

GRANTMAKING FREEDOM IS
A TWO-EDGED SWORD

Freedom is both the grantmaker's greatest strength and potential undoing. Subject to minimal legal restrictions,[14] grantmakers are free to do what they want in whatever way they want. They are not encumbered by rules or precedent.

Unlike the rest of the world, private foundations do not have to raise money or compete in the marketplace. A private foundation will not go bankrupt or get voted out of office because its strategy is misunderstood. It is free to take risks that business, governments, and most individuals cannot afford to take. This freedom, and the independence that comes with it, is the pinnacle of foundation privilege. It allows foundations to reach for the stars, to tackle tough issues with originality and vigor.

However, foundation freedom is a two-edged sword. It permits foundations to fashion a life of ease and comfort if they so choose. Foundations are free to make indiscriminate grants without thought or effort. These grants will be praised by the people receiving the money and lauded by the mainstream media. Criticism is far more likely to be visited on foundations who stick their necks out and try to make a difference.

Critics of foundations have likened them to Lake Wobegon, where all children are above average, and the Galapagos Islands, where there are no natural predators. Foundations can, if they let themselves, live in a bubble. They can avoid the rigors of curiosity and hard work and tell themselves that they are doing a wonderful job. No one will hold them to account. The freedom to choose between the difficult work of good grantmaking and self-deluded bliss is one that challenges even the best of intentions.

FOUNDATION UNDERPERFORMANCE IS COMMON

Dr. Susan Raymond, a distinguished author and speaker on the role of philanthropy in society, has compared foundation grantmakers to "mortgage brokers" who shuffle paper and evaluate grant proposals according to their probability of success, all of which leads them away from the most pressing and difficult issues of the day. She admonishes foundations to come back to the world of ideas, even though there may be no proof of immediate impact.[15]

Bill Somerville, in *Grassroots Philanthropy: Field Notes of a Maverick Grantmaker*, offers this assessment:

> It would seem logical that foundations should be accomplishing things nobody else in American society would even dare to attempt. But collectively we have fallen far short of this mark . . . Despite our freedom to construct institutions that make sense and serve people's needs, foundations more often emulate the worst aspects of big government, with cumbersome regulations, endless forms and arcane bureaucratic procedures . . .
>
> The thought of failure terrifies most funders. With almost nothing to lose, grantmakers persistently embrace safe and predictable projects instead of untested, but promising, new ideas. They confuse bold action with recklessness . . . Year after year, we can make middling, unimaginative grants, budging the world not one iota.[16]

Underperformance in grantmaking is as old as philanthropy itself:

> One of the serious obstacles . . . is indiscriminate charity . . . Of every thousand dollars spent in so called charity today, it

is probable that $950 is unwisely spent . . . as to produce the very evils which it proposes to mitigate or cure . . .

As a rule, the sins [of philanthropists] . . . are because they will not take time to think, and chiefly because it is much easier to give than to refuse . . . The miser millionaire who hoards his wealth does less injury to society than the careless millionaire who squanders his unwisely, even if he does so under cover of the mantle of sacred charity.[17]

The pioneers of American philanthropy believed in a strong work ethic and deplored handouts that would diminish a person's independence. They believed, correctly in my view, that fostering dependence upon grants would debilitate individuals and diminish society. The best grants are those that enable people to help themselves and do not do for them what they can and should do for themselves.

A survey by The Center for Effective Philanthropy (CEP)[18] found that foundation CEOs are their own toughest critics. A majority were critical of their foundation's grantmaking and the impact that it made. Among the impediments cited were cultural and organizational issues within their foundations. An earlier CEP survey found that most foundations had articulated a strategy but did not follow it.[19] This is an old survey, and I would be interested to see if an updated version showed that more foundations are hewing to their strategy.

Underperformance knows no sectoral boundaries. We see it in business, the nonprofit world, and government. Effective grantmaking is more difficult than most business, nonprofit, and government activity. It is perfectly natural that many, perhaps most, grants will fall short of their potential. Rather than bemoan grantmaking that falls short, it is more useful to consider approaches that foundations have used to produce effective grantmaking. Three essentials leap to mind: risk taking, immersion in your field of interest, and strategy.

Build a Culture that Values Risk

Culture starts with the board. In a timid foundation culture, the risk of failure inhibits innovation. Grantmaking results can take years or even decades to appear, but reputations and careers are measured and advanced in months. From that perspective, the short-term win is better, even if it does not produce lasting results. The unconscious drift toward safety is inexorable: passion is whittled away, and ideals are compromised.

In *Think Again*,[20] Adam Grant discusses the benefits when members of a team feel free to take a risk or look foolish. He describes this as psychological safety (see sidebar) and uses The Gates Foundation as an example. It employs some of the world's leading experts and found that these experts were often too intimidated and fearful to take risks and do their best work. The experts worried that a flaw in their work might derail their career. The Gates Foundation hired Adam Grant to help remedy this problem. Grant describes one of the exercises he used to build psychological safety and encourage risk taking. Melinda Gates volunteered to go first:

> Her team compiled criticisms from staff surveys, printed them on note cards, and had her react in real time in front of a camera. She read one employee's complaint that she was like Mary F###ing Poppins—the first time anyone could remember hearing Melinda curse—and explained how she was working on making her imperfections more visible.[21]

The effect was predictable and junior employees saw Melinda as more human and approachable.

The concept of psychological safety can help foundation leaders build a culture that values and rewards originality, independence, and risk taking in grantmaking. Regardless of the foundation's size, if its leaders show humility and the confidence to admit their own ignorance and mistakes, then this will give others the courage to take risks. This feeds grantmaking passion.

Effective foundations value originality and independence even where there is no immediate evidence of impact. Debate is open, rigorous, and lively. Curiosity, creativity, and new ways of doing things are encouraged. Failure is not a thing to be blamed on someone but an opportunity to learn. These values go to the heart of foundation culture and must be deliberately cultivated. Foundation leaders should regularly ask themselves (and their staff, if they have one) whether they honestly aspire to feed grantmaking passion. Do they reward innovation and risk taking? What can they do to improve?

This chart from *Think Again*[22] is an excellent tool for grantmakers. We should all ask ourselves, "Which of these statements are true at my foundation?"

PSYCHOLOGICAL SAFETY

When You Have It	When You Don't
Seeing mistakes as opportunities to learn	Seeing mistakes as threats to your career
Being willing to take risks and fail	Being unwilling to rock the boat
Speaking your mind in meetings	Keeping your ideas to yourself
Openly sharing your struggles	Only touting your strengths
Trusting your teammates and supervisors	Fearing teammates and supervisors
Sticking your neck out	Having your head chopped off

Immerse Yourself in Your Foundation's Field or Fields of Interest

Most grantmakers do not come up with creative ideas and innovative strategies by themselves. They get them from other people. Effective grantmakers immerse themselves in their fields of interest and listen and talk to people who share their mission. Their best ideas are out there waiting for them. Grantees, potential grantees, clients, volunteers, academics, and other experts have lived, studied, and worked with the grantmaker's issues of interest. They possess a wealth of knowledge and ideas. It is the grantmaker's task to find and engage these people, not the other way around. Immersion in one's field of grantmaking yields knowledge and this begets ideas. Knowledge is the stuff of innovation and action. Acquiring knowledge that will lead to ideas and action means finding the right people and building relationships with them.

Finding and meeting people, even when you don't know anybody, is surprisingly easy. I will illustrate with JSF's experience. One of JSF's core missions is to assist Indigenous Peoples to obtain education and employment. When we started, in the early 1990s, we knew little about Indigenous Peoples. We wanted to learn the issues and find out how we might help and who we could work with. We went to reservations in Washington, Arizona, New Mexico, Montana, North and South Dakota, Minnesota, and Wisconsin. When we asked people to meet with us, we were welcomed. People were eager to talk to us and spent hours educating us.

Our visits to the reservations and tribal colleges gave us a picture. We experienced firsthand the beauty and hardship of these places, the small populations, and the vast distances between them. There is no substitute for being there. I vividly remember conversations that took place over twenty years ago, and those early lessons have stayed with me.

After a couple of years, we had gained an awareness of the issues and the organizations and people we could work with. We started to convene meetings on or near reservations. We brought together Indigenous educators and nonprofit leaders and together we began to formulate grantmaking theory and strategy. We concluded that entrepreneurship and business education would be a catalyst for economic growth and employment on reservations. Our first series of grants went to various tribal colleges to fund scholarships for students studying entrepreneurship or business. This program continues to be a mainstay, and we have modified it as we have learned.

One of the collateral benefits of immersion in a foundation's fields of grantmaking is meeting and recruiting potential board members. People working in your field of interest can bring knowledge and experience to your board. Meeting and working with them over time will usually reveal whether they would be a good fit on your board. JSF recruits most of its directors from its grantmaking fields of interest and this has improved the board immeasurably.

Commit to a Strategy

Chapter 5 deals extensively with how to develop a strategy and the reasons to do so. It is enough to say here that strategy gives grantmakers focus and goals. Without strategy, grantmaking is aimless and usually ineffectual. Strategy is never perfect and should evolve as foundations gain experience and learn more about their fields of interest. Regardless of how good it is, strategy is useless if you do not follow it. There will be times when you will be tempted by easier or seemingly more interesting grant opportunities. Resist these distractions and hew to foundation strategy!

GRANTMAKING IS INVESTING

Investing is defined as the "action of investing money for profit or material result."[23] This is the essence of the grant transaction. A foundation makes a grant in the expectation of a result, which will advance its mission. The only thing that distinguishes this from a for-profit investment is that the expected result is for society's benefit, not private gain. The grant's return on investment is social, not financial.[24] This difference makes grantmaking much more difficult, but it is investing nonetheless.

The alternative to the investment characterization is to say that a grant is a gift. I do not find this helpful, for several reasons. First, a gift is freely given with no expectation of anything in return. This is contrary to a philanthropic grant, which both grantee and grantor understand will be used for an agreed purpose. A second, and perhaps larger, problem with the gift characterization is that it implies generosity and the conferring of favor by the grantor. However, generosity plays no part in foundation grants. Foundations are created to make grants and are legally required to do so. When a foundation makes a grant, it is simply conducting its business.

The idea of foundation largesse is not a good footing for a grantor and grantee relationship. Grantees do not enjoy the financial independence of foundations. They usually need grant money to keep the lights on and meet payroll. This gives rise to an unequal bargaining position between foundation and grantee, which must be managed for them to enjoy a trusting, productive relationship.

If you look beyond the parties' inequality of bargaining power, it is easy to see that a grant is not the conferring of favor. The foundation makes a grant, and the grantee recipient does the work. How is this a favor? The foundation's money is useless without a grantee to put it to work. The foundation and the grantee each have something that the other needs. They are partners.

The conceptual framework of financial investing is useful to the grantmaker because it readily conveys the task at hand, which is especially helpful for people who come to philanthropy from other walks of life. When I joined the board of JSF in 1993, I wondered what we would do at grant meetings. We were writing checks. What was there to talk about?[25] I didn't know much about investing an endowment either, but I understood the investor's task of careful study and analysis and that expertise was required. The grantmaker's task is similar, as is the need for a rigorous process. Many of financial investing's principles, models, and processes can be adapted and used by grantmakers. Do not worry that a disciplined investment style process will rob your grantmaking of its life and creativity. A rigorous process will spark your imagination, not constrain it. Investing of any kind—including grantmaking—pays its largest rewards to creativity and independence.

In characterizing grantmaking as investing, I want to make it clear that I do not subscribe to the theory that foundations or nonprofits should be like private businesses, where profitability is the bottom line. Making money and social impact are not correlated. Most nonprofits concentrate on people and issues that do not generate cash returns. Impact is their bottom line, not profitability. If you want to judge the effectiveness of a nonprofit, then you must take the time to understand its mission, operations, and impact. The financial metrics of financial investing do not apply. Nonprofits can be efficiently managed and still lose money.

Consider a potential grantee that cannot balance its budget and will require philanthropic grants for the foreseeable future. This information is virtually meaningless without context. You need a deeper understanding of the potential grantee, what problems it attempts to solve, and how it does so. For example, one of JSF's favorite grantees, Clarke Schools for Hearing and Speech, concentrates on oral communication for the deaf and hard of hearing. Oral communication is more feasible with the advent of digital hearing aids and cochlear implants.

A cochlear implant transmits a signal to the brain, which needs to be interpreted. One must learn and practice this, and satisfactory results are difficult to achieve later in life. The brains of preschool children are more adaptable, however, and with early intervention, results can be dramatic. Young children can become sufficiently adept with cochlear implants to hear, speak, carry a tune, and function proficiently in mainstream schools and society.

Clarke provides instruction and training to children of all ages, but its best results are achieved with those from birth to age five. Unfortunately, these children are not old enough to be eligible for educational funding in most jurisdictions, and their parents usually cannot afford to pay. Obviously, the best course is for Clarke to provide as much preschool training as it can, and to pursue philanthropic grants to defray the cost.

Educational funding reforms may come eventually, but in the meantime the money required to provide this training to deaf and hard of hearing preschoolers will create an operational deficit. This is not evidence of unbusinesslike behavior or unsustainability on the part of Clarke. It is perfectly sustainable if Clarke can attract philanthropic support. For a grantmaker with a mission to assist people with disabilities, Clarke's deficit presents an excellent opportunity.

The "they should be more like business" theory is sometimes used to explain shortcomings in foundation performance. Those critics typically say that foundations should be tougher with grantees and drive hard bargains in exchange for grants. Or foundations should act like venture capitalists and show grantees how to run their organizations. These criticisms are as inappropriate to foundations as they are to nonprofits. Foundations invest to improve society, not to make money. They should emulate successful grantmakers, not private venture capitalists or other businesses.

Understanding grants as investments helps a grantmaker think about risk and reward. Bill Somerville suggests that foundations establish a venture fund for riskier grants. Designate part of your grant budget for high-risk, high-impact projects. This will psychologically prepare your foundation to accept risk and energize its grantmaking.[26] JSF follows a similar approach, although we don't call it that. As the name suggests, JSF makes a lot of grants for scholarships, but these are wholesale, not retail. What I mean is that we make grants to schools, colleges, and universities that then award scholarships to individuals, according to agreed criteria.[27]

About 70 percent of JSF grants are to fund, support, and create scholarship programs. Some of these are edgier than others but granting money to students with financial need is low-risk investing. We feel entitled—obligated, actually—to take some risk with the remaining 30 percent of our grant portfolio, and this has been enshrined in our core values. Some of our riskier grants have not produced meaningful results, some have done reasonably well, and a few have been stellar. The risk profile of our grants suits us. We understand the importance of investing in new ideas and taking risks, but we are value investors at heart. The mix of relatively safe and more risky investments suits JSF's personality.

As a grantmaker, what risk profile will suit your foundation? How does your foundation feel about safety, uncertainty, and failure? There are no right answers, but the foundation should understand its investment personality, and structure its grantmaking portfolio accordingly.

Understanding grants as investments brings home the need for achieving and evaluating results. It is not enough to distribute money to worthy causes. What do you have to show for it? What good are you doing?

Significant difficulties await the practicing grantmaker. Their solution does not require extraordinary skill or wisdom. It is as simple—and as difficult—as understanding the principles of philanthropy and planning, organizing, and diligently attending to your work. Over time, you will accumulate experience and knowledge and get better at it. Good grantmaking is a practice, not an elevated state of being.

2

Seven Stories and Ten Principles

Grantmakers and their nonprofit grantees are intertwined, both in this book and in the practice of philanthropy. Sometimes the line between grantor and grantee is blurred, such as when a grantmaker with special expertise and capacity does more than make grants. For example, an environmentally focused foundation might have the expertise and capacity to conduct research and publish papers, in addition to making grants. In most cases, however, a grantmaker's story needs information about its grantee or grantees for it to make sense. It is the grantees, after all, who put the grant money to work.

MEMORABLE GRANTMAKERS AND GRANTEES

These stories illustrate the discussion in the previous chapter. They show the problems that the grantmakers and grantees set out to remedy and the methods they used. Their different responses to obstacles faced are particularly telling and often spelled the difference between success and failure.

Andrew Carnegie and Public Libraries

Andrew Carnegie has done more for public libraries than anyone before or since. His grantmaking was intended to allow ordinary people to have free access to knowledge and ideas contained in books. During the Great Depression, Carnegie's Washington, DC, library was referred to as "the intellectual breadline."[28] It seems impossible to overestimate the social benefits of his grantmaking. This is all the more so when we consider that present-day libraries go beyond print to include films, audiobooks, Internet, activities, and lectures.

Carnegie's personal story is vintage rags to riches. His family emigrated from Scotland in 1848 with no money. He went to work at age thirteen as a "bobbin boy" in a textile mill for $1.20 per week. Carnegie was smart, self-educated, and inexorable. In 1901 he sold US Steel to J.P. Morgan for $480 million (about $14 billion in today's dollars) and devoted himself to philanthropy.[29]

Carnegie thought of himself as "only a trustee" of his wealth. Unlike Rockefeller's religious conviction, Carnegie's view was based on the clear-eyed realization that the community had helped him to amass his fortune.[30]

Carnegie rejected the idea of leaving large amounts to children and famously declared "the man who dies . . . rich dies disgraced." He was a proponent of large estate taxes to pry wealth from the dead hands of "selfish millionaires." He felt that grantmakers should never do for people what they can and should do themselves: "The main consideration should be to . . . give those who desire to rise the aids by which they may rise; to assist but rarely or never to do all."[31]

With this abiding principle, Carnegie opined on some of the best uses by which philanthropic trustees could help communities. These included universities, libraries, hospitals, public parks, and meeting and concert halls. He noted that there was not, and should not be, consensus on the best fields of philanthropy. Each trustee's heart must be in the work.[32] He described his love of libraries:

> It is, no doubt, possible that my own personal experience may have led me to value a free library beyond all other forms of beneficence. When I was a boy in Pittsburgh, Colonel Anderson, of Allegheny—a name I can never speak without feelings of devotional gratitude—opened his little library of four hundred books to boys. Every Saturday afternoon he was in attendance himself at his house to exchange books. No one but he who has felt it can know the intense longing with which the arrival of Saturday was awaited, that a new book might be had . . . and it was when reveling in these treasures that I resolved if ever wealth came to me, that it should be used to establish free libraries, that other poor boys might receive opportunities similar to those for which we were indebted to that noble man.[33]

Libraries figure prominently in the histories of the world's great societies. In the nineteenth century, most libraries required an annual paid subscription. In the US, the free or public library had its beginnings in Massachusetts, which passed an act in 1848 authorizing the City of Boston to levy a tax for the establishment of a free public library. By 1896, twenty-nine states and the District of Columbia had similar legislation.[34]

Carnegie's library campaign began in earnest in 1901, when he delivered $5.2 million (over $161 million today) in US Steel Bonds to the director of the New York Public Library. It was agreed that Carnegie would fund the building of a 65-branch library system across the five boroughs of New York City and that the City of New York, in return for Carnegie's grant, would provide the sites and staff, maintain the buildings, keep them open and free to the public from 9 a.m. to 9 p.m. every day, and fill them with books.[35]

In Canada, Carnegie funded the building of 125 free public libraries, many of which are still functioning, over one hundred years later. They include landmark buildings, several of which appear on the Canadian Register of historic places. Carnegie is credited with laying the groundwork for the free public library system in Canada and encouraging the thriving spirit of local communities to build greater community connections.[36]

Carnegie got the idea of requiring a local government authority to commit to the entire cost of operating the library from the practice in Great Britain and it became a cornerstone of his strategy. James Bertram, his secretary, describes it in action:

> So [Carnegie] . . . hit upon his scheme to get action out of the public authorities . . . to offer communities a building, on condition that they would fill it with books and tax themselves for its maintenance . . . his real purpose was not to found libraries, himself, but to force the communities to do so.[37]

Carnegie knew more about financing and building public libraries than anyone in the country. He used this knowledge to work with grantee partners toward a common mission. For example, the City of Philadelphia asked Carnegie for a grant to fund a 30-branch library system at a cost of $20,000 to $30,000 per branch. Carnegie pointed out that the branch libraries should be larger and contain lecture rooms. He thought that $50,000 a branch would be more appropriate and offered funding in that amount (double what was requested) provided the city would stock and maintain the libraires.[38] His goal was to create useful public libraries, not to drive hard bargains.

Carnegie spoke of the importance of focus in his grantmaking: "I have seldom or never known a great success made by a jack of all trades, the board member in twenty companies, the controller of none. I am in the library manufacturing business and beg to be allowed to concentrate my time upon it until it is filled."[39]

Carnegie's library grantmaking is remarkable for its execution. Carnegie made grants of $41 million (well over $1 billion in today's dollars) and funded the construction of 2,504 public libraries in the United States, Canada, the United Kingdom, and other countries around the world.[40]

Carnegie used his business experience and knowledge to develop his strategy, which he executed objectively and meticulously. He built a system, which was described by his biographer:

> [Carnegie] and Bertram had designed their own scientific, corporate system of giving, one that guarded against sentiment and made decisions based on hard data about population, taxation, and site availability. The benefit of such a program was that it did not overwhelm Carnegie with details and small-scale decision making. His staff, knowing clearly what he intended to pay for, followed his instructions

as precisely as they could, without bothering him. He had turned his giving into a business—a very efficient one.[41]

This story illustrates the idea of immersion in and knowledge of your field of interest. It also illustrates the value of strategy and focus in grantmaking and executing this strategy in a businesslike way. In Carnegie's words, his grantmaking was "the library manufacturing business." The strategy and systems that he developed enabled him to achieve prodigious results in a relatively short time. He was able to use the ideas and practices of those who went before him and accomplish more in this field than anyone before or since.

Admiral Peary, the American Museum of Natural History, and Minik

Admiral Robert Peary was an Arctic explorer and, in his day, a household name. A US postage stamp has been made in his honor. He worked closely with the American Museum of Natural History in New York (the museum), which had a stable of wealthy grantors and was itself a funder of scientific expeditions and a buyer of artifacts. The president of the museum was Morris Jesup, a wealthy philanthropist and benefactor of both Peary and the museum.

In 1897, Peary mounted an expedition to Greenland. He had made previous expeditions to Greenland and had brought back artifacts for the museum. These artifacts were important to the museum because it wanted to build an Arctic exhibit. No other institution in America had one of any significance.

Peary and the museum had set their sights on the Cape York meteorite, one of the largest meteorites anywhere in the world. For centuries, it had been the sole source of iron tools for the Inuit and, if Peary could dislodge it and get it to New York, it would make an impressive exhibit. The museum also asked Peary to bring back an "Eskimo" for observation and study. Peary needed money and scientific validation for his expeditions and the museum was a vital source of both.

On September 30, 1897, Peary's ship, *The Hope*, arrived back from Greenland and docked in Brooklyn. The press had been alerted and there was great fanfare. A crowd of thirty thousand people paid twenty-five cents each to marvel at the meteorite, polar bear cubs, and, best of all, six live Inuit.[42]

Within months, four of the six Inuit had died from pneumonia and/or tuberculosis. One of the two survivors was Minik, a seven-year-old boy who had accompanied his father, Qisuk, on the trip and had been orphaned by his death. He grew up in New York, neither American nor Inuk, and lived a short, unhappy life.[43] If this seems a tragic misadventure, the real story is worse.

From the perspectives of Peary and the museum, the trip was successful. Peary had enhanced his stature through favorable public notice and further ingratiated himself with the museum and the philanthropist, Morris Jesup. All of this put him on a better footing to pursue his main objective, being the first person to reach the North Pole. Later, Peary was able to negotiate a price of $40,000, paid to him personally for "his" meteorite.[44] Jesup helped found the Peary Arctic Club and became its first president.

The museum got the thirty-seven-ton Cape York meteorite to include in its burgeoning Arctic exhibit. The fact that it had been an Inuit treasure made it even more desirable. It also got other exhibits, including the mortal remains of the four Inuit who had died. The story of Qisuk's remains is particularly telling.

After Qisuk died, the museum wanted to dissect his body and display his bones, but it knew that this would not be acceptable to his son, Minik, or the other Inuit. The museum's solution was to stage a sham interment, which would trick seven-year-old Minik into thinking that his father had received a proper burial. The museum superintendent, William Wallace, later described it:

> That night some of us gathered on the museum grounds by order of the scientific staff, and got an old log about the length of a human corpse. This was wrapped in cloth, a mask attached to one end of it, and all was in readiness.
>
> Dusk was the time chosen for the mock burial, as there was some fear of attracting too much attention from the street, which might invite an investigation that would prove disastrous. Then, too, the boy would be less apt to discover the ruse. The funeral party knew the act must be accomplished quickly and quietly. So, about the time the lights began to flare Minik was taken out on the grounds, where the imitation body was placed on the ground and a mound of stones piled on top of it after the Eskimo fashion.
>
> While Minik stood sobbing by, the museum men lingered around watching the proceedings. The thing worked well. The boy never suspected ...
>
> When he got back to the other Eskimos, he told them he had seen his father buried, and they were satisfied.[45]

Years later Minik saw Qisuk's bones on display at the museum and asked to have them so he could bury them. The museum refused.

Minik took his story to the press, and in 1907 *The New York World*, Joseph Pulitzer's paper, published it under the headline "Give Me My Father's Body." It gave a scathing account of the entire affair. Two years later, Minik's story was also headlined in the *San Francisco Examiner*. Throughout it all, the museum kept Qisuk's bones. In 1993, when the museum faced renewed publicity and pressure it finally relented. Qisuk's bones, and those of the three other Inuit, were sent home to Greenland.[46]

Minik's version of these events is heart wrenching:

> At the start Peary was kind enough to my people. He made them presents of ornaments, a few knives and guns for hunting, and wood to build sledges. But as soon as he was ready to start home his other work began.
>
> Before our eyes he packed up the bones of our dead friends and ancestors. To the women's crying and the men's questioning he answered that he was taking our dead friends to a warm and pleasant land to bury them. Our sole supply of flint for lighting and iron for hunting and cooking implements was furnished by a huge meteorite. This Peary put aboard his steamer and took from my poor people, who needed it so much. After this he coaxed my father and that brave man Natooka, who were the staunchest hunters and wisest heads for our tribe, to go with him to America.
>
> Our people were afraid to let them go, but Peary promised them that they should have Natooka and my father back within a year, and that with them would come a great stock of

guns and ammunition and wood and metal and presents for the women and children . . .

We were crowded into the hold of the vessel and treated like dogs. Peary seldom came near us. When we reached the end of the sea voyage, we were given the most miserable and unhealthy quarters on the steamship Kite, and lay off Brooklyn for several days on exhibition.

After this we were sent to the Museum of Natural History in New York. There we were quartered in a damp cellar most unfavorable to people from the dry air of the North. One after another we became ill and began to die off; during the fourth month my poor father died . . .

You can imagine how closely that brought us together: how our disease and suffering and lack of understanding of all the strange things around us, and the ominous death of the three other Eskimo of our party, who one by one bade us a sad farewell, made us sit tremblingly waiting our turn to go—more and more lonesome and alone, hopelessly far from home, we grew to depend on one another, and to love each other as no father and son under ordinary conditions could possibly love . . .

Oh, they have given me a thousand deaths! When I could be of no further use to them and my illness frightened them, they turned me adrift—and yet I am not dead. I wish I was, I wish I was![47]

If you think that Minik's story is just a tale from a bygone era and cannot happen today, think again. Social attitudes and conventions change with the times, but human nature does not. The desire for money can be a powerful motivating force, and the grantmaker must always be alert to this. Ill-conceived grants usually do not kill people, but they often influence them to abandon useful work and pursue activity that is not useful or that they are unqualified to undertake.

This story illustrates the importance of careful thought and planning, both in choice of a grantee partner and in execution of an idea. It is a cautionary tale of the power of money and the unintended consequences of reckless grantmaking. The decision to bring Inuit from their native Greenland to New York was ill conceived, and the arrangements for their housing and care in New York were inadequate. The tragic death of four of the six Inuit and the ruination of a fifth, were the unintended consequences. Grantmakers must be mindful of the power of money and the need to use it responsibly.

The Dorr Foundation and Highway Safety

It is the quality of grants and the strategy behind them that determine their effectiveness, not their size. Consider the impact of the Dorr Foundation,[48] which has assets of $7.5 million and an annual grant budget of about $350,000. Currently it supports the development of new and innovative science curricula or programs at elementary grade levels through college. It also supports special education projects for youth relating to conservation and the environment. It was founded by John Dorr, a renowned metallurgical engineer, to support scientific work in the fields of chemistry and metallurgy.

In the early 1950s, John Dorr became interested in highway safety. His wife had observed that motorists would either "hug the center line or swerve away from it in the face of oncoming traffic"[49] at night, particularly when the road was dark and wet with rain. Dorr believed that a white line along the edge of the highway would help motorists stay oriented and thereby reduce accidents. He took his idea to the Connecticut highway authority and was ignored.

Dorr wrote to a local newspaper, outlined his idea, identified a stretch of road for a test site and offered to fund it. The Connecticut highway authority conducted a test on a strip of the Merritt Parkway and found that an outside line "improved automobile position in the center of the lane"[50] and would reduce accidents and wear and tear on highway shoulders. The entire highway was striped with an outside line. The State of New York followed by continuing the outside line along a test strip on the Hutchinson River Parkway, which meets the Merritt Parkway at the state border. Accidents were reduced, but attribution was more difficult because of an increase in police presence on the Parkway.

Painting outside lines on highways is an added expense, and new ideas, even good ones, are not always accepted easily. Highway authorities across the country did not go down without a fight. Some ventured that the new lines would be a distraction. Some said that drivers might try to drive to the right of the outside lines and go off the road. Others said that the lines were ineffectual. Some said that they worked only on highways with paved shoulders. Others said that the lines would only work on highways without paved shoulders. Outside lines were deemed "highly controversial"[51] in the late 1950s.

John Dorr persisted. The Dorr Foundation funded comprehensive studies in Rhode Island, New Jersey, and Connecticut, overseen by the Highway Research Board of the National Academy of Sciences. Evidence from the studies and testing supported the outside line. The Dorr Foundation became a source for information on tests and evidence proving the efficacy of outside lines on highways. It printed and circulated materials and participated, through John Dorr, in committees and groups including the President's Action Committee for Traffic Safety, the Highway Research Board of the National Academy of Sciences, and the Federal Bureau of Public Roads. Within a few years of Dorr's committing himself and the Dorr Foundation to this cause, outside lines gained "universal acceptance and application."[52]

This story illustrates many grantmaking lessons. The most obvious is that impact depends more upon persistence, adherence to a strategy, and knowledge than a foundation's size or lack of staff. In fact, the Dorr Foundation's small size was an advantage because it allowed it to quickly alter its strategy and field of interest. Measurement of results and advocacy were vital aspects of Dorr's strategy. More than anything, this story illustrates the power of foundation individualism and freedom. John Dorr created the foundation to further science education. He saw a different opportunity, immersed himself and his foundation in it, and catalyzed change on a grand scale.

The Ford Foundation and Commonfund

In the 1960s, higher education was the major focus of the Ford Foundation's grantmaking. The foundation needed to reduce this grantmaking but knew that colleges and universities relied upon it. In 1969 it approved a $2.8 million grant to establish the Commonfund, "a co-operative undertaking of educational institutions to improve the productivity of endowments." This was a nonprofit organization that would invest higher education endowments with the same strategies and skills as used in professional investment firms.[53]

The Commonfund grant has been described as one of the most successful grants ever made by a foundation. It transformed investment management by higher education and generated more new wealth for higher education than Ford Foundation grants. Twenty-five years later, the Commonfund had over 1,200 members and $14 billion under management, and in 2023, it was still going strong. This story exhibits the knowledge, originality, thought, and creativity of good grantmaking.

In the Ford Foundation's 1966 annual report, its new president, McGeorge Bundy, expressed concern about the financial future of higher education and noted that investment management could be improved. Even a 1 percent annual increase in investment return would produce more than double what Ford was granting to higher education.[54]

The Teachers Insurance and Annuity Association (TIAA) had also thought about higher education's poor investment returns and had conceived the idea of a mutual fund for colleges and universities. When they read the Ford Foundation's annual report, two of TIAA's senior officials met with Bundy and discussed their idea of a mutual fund. Bundy liked the idea but wisely deferred action. Instead, the Ford Foundation engaged grantees in discussions and made two grants to fund studies on the legal and management aspects of higher education investment.

Representatives of higher education grantees formed part of a study group that produced *Managing Educational Endowments*, a 1969 report to the Ford Foundation, which quantified higher education investment underperformance at almost 6 percent annually.[55] After receiving the study and getting widespread support from grantees, the Ford Foundation made a grant to establish the Commonfund.

This story illustrates the power of knowledge and how good grantmaking can serve as a catalyst to help grantees to become more independent. Ford did not create or even suggest the Commonfund. It gave its grantee partners the means to do so themselves. Nor did Ford use its financial power to impose its name or control on the new organization. It recognized that the institutions that benefited from Commonfund should own and manage it. For university and college endowments, Ford's grants had a ripple effect far beyond the grantees directly affected. They led the way for similar changes in investing for endowments in the United States, Canada, and other parts of the developed world.

Operation Smile and Smile Train

Bill Magee, a plastic and orofacial surgeon, and his wife, Kathy, a nurse and social worker, founded Operation Smile in 1982. The idea was to send volunteer flying surgical missions from the United States to developing countries to perform corrective surgery on children born with cleft lip and cleft palate. Without treatment, these children would face a lifetime of health-related problems and, much worse, of being social outcasts.

Corrective surgery is usually simple, but most families in developing countries did not have enough money to pay for it. As a result, children born with cleft lip and cleft palate were untreated.

What a difference Operation Smile made. What leverage! A 15-minute operation would greatly improve a person's quality of life forever. A grantmaker could hardly do better, right?

The desire to save children from a miserable life is laudable and has a strong emotional pull. Once one gets into the details, however, it becomes murkier. Flying Western surgical missions into developing countries can violate a basic premise— namely, doing for other people what they can and should do themselves.

In the early 1990s, Brian Mullaney was an advertising executive in New York, and among his clients were cosmetic surgeons on the Upper East Side of Manhattan. He rode the subway and, when school let out, so did thousands of school children. He noticed that some of them had cleft lips and other deformities.

Mullaney's work had taught him the power of plastic surgery, and he started an organization to connect underserved children who had facial deformities with the surgeons who could help them. Before long, every hospital in New York City was helping to provide free corrective surgery to underserved children. The New York Board of Education then took up the cause. Mullaney incorporated a nonprofit and called it Operation Smile.

Later, Brian Mullaney read about Bill and Kathy Magee and their Operation Smile. He flew to Virginia to meet them and took a seat on their board. Mullaney started to fly on Operation Smile's missions to developing countries. The routine was always the same. Three or four hundred children would show up and be examined. Then a list of ninety or one hundred children would be posted, like the roster of a sports team. These were the ones who had made the cut, who would get surgery. The rest were turned away. Their mothers would beg, cry, and throw themselves on the ground. It was heartbreaking, but there seemed no other way.

What kind of organization turns away three hundred children for every hundred it serves? Mullaney thought that there must be a better business model. While in Vietnam on a mission, Mullaney asked a volunteer American surgeon, "Why don't the Vietnamese doctors perform cleft surgery?" The surgeon replied that they do and are better at it than Americans, because they do more of them. Brian asked what Vietnamese surgeons earn and the American doctor told him about $300 a month. Mullaney observed that Operation Smile could pay Vietnamese surgeons to perform cleft surgery on everyone who needed it, and it would cost less than what they were presently paying to treat a third of them. The American surgeon agreed but asked, "What would I do?"

Mullaney continued to pursue the idea of building local capacity. One of his advertising clients was Charles B. Wang, the co-founder and CEO of Computer Associates International. Mullaney pitched the "local surgeon" variation of Operation Smile to him, and he loved it. Wang joined the board of Operation Smile and pledged $10 million to start the new idea, which had been dubbed "Smile Train." Tom Brokaw, of NBC News, got Brian on the *Today Show* and connected him with Bill Gates, who gave $1 million. They envisioned a train going around China, stopping for a couple of weeks to provide training and support for local doctors, and then moving on to the next community.[56]

Operation Smile reportedly sidetracked the Smile Train idea for another initiative, the World Journey of Hope, which involved leasing a flying hospital from evangelist Pat Robertson and conducting a nine-week tour of thirteen countries to treat 5,300 children. The idea was costly (about $9 million, with almost $1 million for promotion and public relations) and not well received within the Operation Smile organization.[57]

Around that time, Operation Smile came under heavy criticism for "assembly line" practices and shoddy, unsafe work, which resulted in higher mortality and poor outcomes, some of which required remediation by local surgeons. A child died in Beijing and an American medical volunteer charged that "it was the direct result of a poorly run mission with far too much attention being paid to publicity and not enough to patient safety and standard monitoring techniques." The death could have been prevented by a standard (and available) monitoring device, which had not been used.[58]

Charles Wang, Brian Mullaney, and others left the board of Operation Smile. The parting was anything but amicable. Mullaney and Wang took their Smile Train idea (and Wang's $10 million pledge) and formed a new organization. By then it was clear to them—and many others—that the model of flying medical missions to underdeveloped countries to perform surgery was expensive and bred dependence. Bypassing local governments and physicians also bred resentment, and Operation Smile was criticized for neocolonialism.[59]

Smile Train's strategy was to build local capacity. Local doctors do not have to leave and go back home. Once capacity is built, they are there to perform surgery on anyone who needs it. The cost is a fraction of what it takes to fly doctors from other countries. Further, local doctors, once trained, can train other local doctors. Helping to build local capacity is more agreeable to host countries, and this allowed Smile Train to work with foreign governments and health authorities.[60]

Smile Train's capacity-building model was a game changer, and the number of cleft surgeries increased exponentially. In twenty years, Smile Train estimates that it has reached over one and a half million children in ninety countries. By contrast, Operation Smile reached fewer than 135,000 children in its first twenty-seven years.[61]

Operation Smile's strategy has evolved to emphasize local capacity building. It now recognizes "that people in low-resource environments are more than capable . . . All they need are the resources to make it happen."[62] About 80 percent of its medical missions comprise people from the countries served.

The success of Operation Smile and Smile Train has inspired grant-makers in developing countries to get behind this issue. The outlook for children born with cleft deformities has improved, and it is estimated that 90 percent of them will get the surgery they need within a year.

Smile Train has become a charity juggernaut. Its website features a photo of a young child with a cleft lip and the nearly irresistible plea "Donate Now and Change a Child's Life Forever."[63] However, Smile Train has accumulated a large surplus. The most recent annual report (2021) on its website discloses annual revenue of $213 million, expenses of $147 million, and net assets of $427 million. Surplus assets would fund its operations for years without any further donations.[64] Brian Mullaney left Smile Train in 2011. Charles Wang died in 2018.

This story illustrates how ideas germinate and progress. The local capacity model occurred after years of practicing in the field with the flying missions model. Without

*Operation Smile, there would be no Smile Train. The role
of grantmakers was instrumental in this progression. A
new idea is a beginning and progress occurs while doing.
Practice and experience generate refinements or even complete makeovers. It does not require brilliance. It requires
immersion and application to the task, which is the practice
of grantmaking.*

*This story also illustrates the need for grantmakers to keep
up with the constantly changing landscape of their field of
interest. A cause or an organization that was a good investment ten years ago may no longer be such. Foundations must
be knowledgeable and informed of developments in their
fields of grantmaking and adjust strategy and grantmaking
accordingly.*

Gates Foundation and Small Schools (2000–2009)

The Small Schools Initiative was an attempt to improve high schools
by making them smaller. In a press release announcing a "small schools"
grant, Tom Ark, executive director of education at The Gates Foundation declared in 2003 that "young people who attend smaller schools
that provide a rigorous, personalized education and enable close relationships with adults are more likely to graduate and continue their
education."[65]

The theory seemed plausible, even likely, and The Gates Foundation
invested hundreds of millions in schools across the country.
Governments and other foundations followed its lead.

In 2009, The Gates Foundation's evaluations showed that small schools had not significantly improved student performance. It abandoned the strategy to focus on Common Core and improving teacher performance.

Was the small school's initiative a good bet on a reasonable theory that just didn't work out?

In a 2016 article, "Small Schools: The Edu-Reform Failure That Wasn't," Professor Jack Schneider persuasively makes the case that small schools work:

> As it turns out, small schools do exactly what you might expect. Smallness can create more opportunities for young people to be known, both by one another and by the adults in the building. The relative intimacy of small schools can foster trusting, caring, and attentive relationships.[66]

Professor Schneider cites independent third-party research that found a 9.5 percent increase in graduation at small schools in New York City, which led to higher college enrollments. Another study found similar results in Chicago.

The problem, argues Schneider, is that small schools were viewed as a silver bullet instead of one aspect of a complex issue. And when they didn't deliver dramatic results, their backers declared them a failure and moved on to the next big idea. Had the implementation been more nuanced and the expectations more reasonable, the small schools movement might have turned out differently.

Professor Schneider's plea to foundations and policy elites resonates:

> We need to reimagine the role of the education change-maker. Our schools don't need disrupters, armed with grand notions

about transformation; they need facilitators capable of building capacity. Rather than deciding what works and taking it to scale, we need donors and policy leaders who are interested in helping to strengthen schools and districts, encouraging experimentation, and facilitating the kinds of small changes that add up to big ones.

[It] . . . may not be as sexy as finding scalable solutions. "Small change" is a less enchanting battle cry than "paradigm shift." But . . . gradual progress, frustrating though it can be, is infinitely preferable to perpetual churn.[67]

This story illustrates the difficulty of ambitious grantmaking and the need to persevere, even when there is no evidence of results. Difficult problems are almost always accompanied by commensurate difficulty in measuring their impact. In this case, there was evidence of improvement at some schools but not in others. But the data did not disclose the reason. Several years later, studies revealed that small schools did work in some cities. But by then The Gates Foundation and its partners had moved on. Had they persevered, they might have decided that small schools were part of a more complex solution than they had originally envisioned. Tackling difficult issues is the highest use of foundation freedom. Grantmakers who do so must have patience and realistic expectations. There is usually no simple answer or silver bullet. More likely the answer will be a painstaking and iterative process.

Rockefeller Institute for Medical Research (now The Rockefeller University)

Let us return to the beleaguered Mr. Rockefeller. In 1901 he began a series of grants to establish and support Rockefeller Institute for Medical Research (RIMR), the first biomedical research center in the United States. Rockefeller was well into his philanthropic endeavor by this time and steeped in the fields of education and medicine.

In the late 1880s Rockefeller met Frederick T. Gates, a former Baptist minister, while he was negotiating a series of grants to establish the University of Chicago. He was impressed by Gates's good sense and business acumen and hired him to help with his philanthropic mission. Gates proved to be the perfect "right hand man." He was passionate, had keen intelligence and vision, expressed himself clearly, and, perhaps most important, understood Rockefeller's temperament and methods.[68]

Rockefeller first raised with Gates the idea of a medical research center in the 1890s.[69] Gates was initially receptive to the idea. He had witnessed medicine's futility firsthand in his years as a minister visiting the sick and dying.[70] In those days American medicine was backward and little training was required to enter the profession:

> The country's medical schools were mostly commercial operations, taught by practicing doctors who picked up spare money by lecturing on the side. Standards were so abysmal that many schools did not even require a college degree for entry. Since these medical mills had no incentive to undertake serious research, medicine hovered in a twilight area between science and guesswork.[71]

Gates came back to the idea of a medical research center in 1897, after reading *Principles and Practice of Medicine* by Canadian physician William Osler. The book was an impressive and highly regarded compendium of the latest medical knowledge, but what struck Gates was how little was known:

> [It] . . . absolutely astounded and appalled me [that] . . . the best medical practice did not . . . cure more than four or five diseases . . . It became clear to me that medicine could hardly hope to become a science until medicine should be endowed and qualified men could give themselves to uninterrupted study and investigation . . . entirely independent of practice. To this end, it seemed to me, an institute of medical research ought to be established in the United States.[72]

Gates took up the cause with religious fervor. He prepared a memorandum for Rockefeller urging the establishment of a medical research institute in the style of the Pasteur Institute in Paris, founded in 1888, and the Koch Institute in Berlin, founded in 1891.

If the opportunity for medical research was ripe in the United States, this view was not universally shared by the medical establishment. Pure laboratory research centers did not exist and the idea of gathering medical researchers under one roof and giving them free rein seemed far-fetched:

> The conception of an institution devoted purely to research seemed crackbrained to "common sense." Did not discoveries and inventions appear in a flash of inspiration like (as popular legends taught) Fulton's flash when he saw a kettle boil or Newton's when an apple fell from a tree onto his head?

For their part, academics were afraid that scientific inspiration would not come when called: if they abandoned the comforting routine of teaching, they might well find themselves flapping in the void.[73]

Rockefeller moved with painstaking caution. He made a series of inquiries to explore the feasibility of a medical research center and gradually assembled a small group of medical experts. The group included William Welch, a renowned pathologist who was unofficially known as the "chief counselor in American medicine."[74] Welch was enthusiastic about a research center and agreed to lead the group.

In June 1901, RIMR was incorporated and Welch became the first chair of its board of scientific directors. RIMR began by granting fellowships to researchers at other laboratories in the United States and Europe. This disgusted Frederick Gates, who was impatient to build an independent laboratory. However, there were important issues to resolve, and the research grants allowed the board to keep its options open. Would RIMR be part of a university? What would be its size and scope? Who would direct it?

Theobald Smith, a Harvard professor and member of the board, was the first choice. He refused, citing work commitments. Welch then approached Simon Flexner, who had been his protégé at Johns Hopkins. Flexner was thirty-nine years old, possessed no independent means, and held a prestigious life appointment as head of pathology at the University of Pennsylvania. Welch feared that Flexner might be reluctant to leave it for such a speculative venture.

It would certainly be a leap of faith. While trying to make up his mind, Flexner asked Frederick Gates why he and Rockefeller thought that a medical research laboratory would discover new and useful medical knowledge. Gates replied simply, "Because we have the faith of fools."[75]

Flexner also had his personal doubts. He wrote to Llewellyn Barker, his best friend and confidant and requested advice on a matter "about which I am pretty undecided":

> Am I the man for the place, have I the originality to keep it going, and the physical strength and temperamental qualities? . . . The undertaking is so important for the future medical progress of the country, and so vast in itself that I cannot but view it with some misgiving . . . If I should follow my inclinations, there is no doubt of my accepting. But is it best?[76]

Ultimately, Flexner could not resist the opportunity. He was elected as RIMR's first director in September 1902 and proved to be the perfect choice. One of Flexner's conditions for accepting was a broad mandate for RIMR, "to cover the whole field of medical research in respect both to men and animals."[77] This aligned perfectly with Rockefeller's aspirations. Rockefeller envisioned an institute where the best medical scientists would be given the freedom to define their own priorities and pursue them. Rockefeller wanted "able men with ideas, imagination and courage to put it into productive use."[78]

Flexner was given a one-year leave of absence to travel abroad to observe the work and organization of European research laboratories. He was particularly struck by advice from Anton Dohrn, director of the Naples Zoological Society:

> "Men work here in a dozen different branches of biological science," Dohrn told him. "Can I be an authority on them all?

No, no. Give them perfect freedom. Let them search where and how they will. Help in every way you can, but do not pretend to be master of them . . . Unless you permit workers in the medical institute to make perfect fools of themselves," he warned Flexner, "you will make no great discoveries."[79]

Upon his return Flexner busied himself with plans for a new building and setting up the laboratory. He recruited some of the best scientific minds of his day. Samuel Meltzer, a distinguished pathologist, had left Germany because, as a Jew, he could not hope for a university chair. Flexner offered him a part-time position to start and was somewhat surprised that he accepted. He told Flexner, "I have always paid laboratories to be permitted to work in them; now you propose to pay me to work. Of course, I will come."[80]

Another of Flexner's recruits was Phoebus Aaron Theodor Levene, a Russian-born biochemist who had also studied under Emile Fischer in Berlin. Flexner also recruited his former student from the University of Pennsylvania Hideyo Noguchi, a rice farmer's son from Japan.

Flexner delegated his scientific freedom to the medical experts that he recruited, and it continued to be RIMR's trademark and strength:

[Flexner] . . . selected his staff to represent the broadest base of scientific inquiry, making no attempt to fashion the Institute after his own particular interests. Nor did he press for immediate results. But while publicly asserting that "there is no royal road to discovery," privately he harbored doubts. "The first years," he later confessed, "were nervous ones for all concerned." He felt pressed to deliver himself some important and highly visible result.[82]

Flexner got his opportunity to shine. In 1904, there was an outbreak of cerebrospinal meningitis in New York. There had been earlier outbreaks, but this was by far the worst, killing over one thousand people that year; the mortality rate was 75 percent.

When the outbreak continued into 1905, the City Board of Health appointed a commission to study it, and Flexner was a member. The number of deaths increased, and the commission found no answers.[83] Flexner and RIMR continued to study meningitis and developed a serum to treat it. In 1908 he presented a paper analyzing four hundred individual cases treated with the "Flexner serum" and was able to conclude that it "greatly diminished ... fatalities."[84] Flexner and RIMR were launched, and they never looked back.

Over the next several years, RIMR produced and distributed the Flexner serum free of charge. Until the advent of antibiotics, it was the only effective treatment for cerebrospinal meningitis. Flexner also discovered the viral origins of polio and its mode of transmission and set out the conceptual framework for a polio vaccine, which came decades later.

Hideyo Noguchi became a master microbiologist and pathologist and made breakthroughs in the study of syphilis, which was incurable at the time, and yellow fever, for which he received worldwide recognition.

There were dead ends and failures. Alexis Carrel had a "mousery" built and stocked with fifty-five thousand mice so that he could study the effects of diet on the development of cancer. After a while, the house and its occupants quietly disappeared, with no explanation and no known results.[85] Later, Carrel won a Nobel Prize in Medicine, the first awarded to an American, and the first of nineteen that would be awarded to scientists associated with RIMR.[86]

Flexner, himself exacting and disciplined, embraced the creative freedom of RIMR's scientists and accommodated the confusion that sometimes went with it:

> He wrote about a day in the laboratory when a number of his group were "working merrily" and of how he "caught the spirit and puttered among some embers of studies." Suddenly he observed something through the microscope that he had not seen before. "Nature is a tantalizing mistress . . . and gives her fruits only at particular seasons, when the spirit is on her—and you."[87]

In 1910, Rockefeller created an endowment and RIMR was reorganized so that it could hold and invest these funds. Recognizing that control of the purse meant control of the research agenda, RIMR's annual budget was entrusted to a committee controlled by the scientific directors. Flexner stated:

> Rockefeller and his advisers agreed to a delegation of power such as may never before have existed in an American philanthropic institution. The trustees agreed merely to take care of the funds, leaving the decision of how they were to be spent to a joint committee containing a majority of scientists.[88]

For a grantmaker who wanted to improve the lot of humanity, to seek solutions to long-standing problems, RIMR must have seemed the pinnacle of success. Rockefeller observed to his son, John, Jr.: "If in all our giving, we had never done more than has been achieved by the fine, able, honest men of the Medical Institute, it would have justified all the money and all the effort we have spent."[89]

In 1900, the average life expectancy was roughly half of what it is today. People lived in fear of diseases such as tuberculosis, polio, and pneumonia. Something as simple as a cold or an infection could turn deadly. Cancer was a death sentence. There was little hope of improvement because there was no organized effort toward scientific progress.

Rockefeller's grantmaking was the catalyst that changed everything. RIMR was the beginning of a new era of scientific research and evidence-driven medicine. The United States emerged as a world leader in medical research, and the benefits to humanity continue to increase exponentially.

The great Winston Churchill gave a world perspective on RIMR when he referred to Rockefeller's endowment of medical research as a "milestone of progress for the human race."[90] For the practicing philanthropist, the assessment of Ron Chernow is more useful, if less momentous:

> The fiercest robber baron had turned out to be the foremost philanthropist. Rockefeller accelerated the shift from the personal, ad hoc charity that had traditionally been the province of the rich to something more powerful and more impersonal. He established the promotion of knowledge, especially scientific knowledge, as a task no less important than giving alms to the poor or building schools, hospitals, and museums. He showed the value of expert opinion, thorough planning, and competent administration in nonprofit work, setting a benchmark for professionalism in the emerging foundation field.[91]

This story illustrates the necessity for a strategy that is based on knowledge, experience, and analysis. Rockefeller had been immersed in the fields of education and medicine for years. It also illustrates the power of listening to grantees and giving them the tools that they need, not the tools that you think they need. Rockefeller recognized and deferred to the superior knowledge of his experts and grantees; he never meddled in their work or tried to claim credit for it.

TEN PRINCIPLES

The following principles are all suggested in the seven stories. They include the essential elements discussed in the previous chapter and serve as a summary of both chapters.

1. Grants Are Investments

Bring the "urgency and focus" of the business world to your grantmaking.[92] Whether you are making grants yourself or acting through staff, grantmaking activity must be purposeful and organized. Treat your grants like the precious investments they are.

Whatever your size, learn from the example of Andrew Carnegie. He was able to "manufacture" almost three thousand libraries because he knew his business and went about it in an organized efficient manner.

Your business and investing are different from the for-profit world. Financial success is uncorrelated to the quality of your grantmaking or grantee partners. Your return is social benefit, not profit, and your strategies will be different.

For instance, Andrew Carnegie did not try to drive hard bargains to squeeze more out of his grantee partners. Nor did he lavish money on them. His strategy was to build public libraries for municipalities who agreed to fill them with books and pay for their operations and maintenance. He followed his strategy in a focused and businesslike fashion.

2. Knowledge Is a Vital Foundation Asset

Foundation leaders should immerse themselves in their fields of interest. It is the best way to learn. This is where your ideas will come from. Knowledge and ideas will inform your strategy and make it better. Learning and getting better are at the heart of good grantmaking practice.

Whether it operates around a kitchen table or through a staff, your foundation needs to get outside, to meet the organizations in its fields of interest and the people that they serve. The volunteers, academics, and professionals who live and work in these fields have something to tell you. Go out and talk to them. Ask them to serve on your foundation's board and committees. They will bring passion and knowledge.

Knowledge always precedes great grantmaking. All the great grantmaking stories—Carnegie, Dorr, Ford, Rockefeller—exhibit the power of immersion in a field of interest and resultant knowledge.

3. Grantmaking Is an Iterative Process

Great ideas do not usually arrive in their final form. They build on each other and improve. The story of Operation Smile and Smile Train illustrates the iterative nature of the grantmaking process. Performing remedial surgery in underdeveloped countries led to the idea of empowering surgeons in these countries. The practice of good grantmaking leads to better grantmaking.

Knowledgeable grantmakers can play a big part in the iterative process of ideas and can help propel the evolution of strategy.

4. Choose Grantees Carefully and Show Them Deference

Realize that grantees do the work of advancing your foundation's mission, and you need them as much as they need you. You invest, they work. Two things follow from this. You should choose grantees carefully and treat them with respect.

Choosing a grantee partner is one of the most important and difficult tasks in grantmaking. The execution of your foundation's strategy depends upon the quality of its grantee partners. If grantees cannot execute, then the grant will be ineffectual, regardless of strategy.

The second point, treating grantee partners with respect, seems trite, but surveys show that many foundations do not do so. Respect usually means deference for a grantee's superior knowledge. Grantees usually know their business better than foundation grantors. Grantees are the teachers and foundations are the students. Foundations should ask, not tell.

Rockefeller's grants to RIMR illustrate the deference and respect of a sophisticated grantmaker. After Rockefeller created RIMR, he entrusted its agenda to medical experts. He understood that success would depend upon these "fine, able" people and that his job was not to control them but to enable them to do their work.

Trust is the basis for deep conversations on mission and strategy. With trust, a grantee partner will often want insight and advice from an experienced partner. On the other hand, if the grantee sees its relationship with a foundation as a cat and mouse game (with a grant as the prize) there will be no trust and no deep conversations about mission.

5. Give Grantees the Tools

The best grants are those that empower people and organizations to be more independent. Grants provide the "aids," as Carnegie put it, by which people can help themselves. Neither foundations nor nonprofits should do for others what they can and should do for themselves.

The Ford Foundation's grant to establish Commonfund is a good example. The foundation understood that management of higher education endowments could be improved and had a good idea to do it. But it did not try to implement this solution on behalf of its grantees. Instead, it provided funding so that they could study the issue and come to their own conclusion. Then it provided a grant to enable them to establish Commonfund.

The grantees were the owners and operators of Commonfund and this enabled them to invest more successfully. These investment gains produced more new wealth than the grants they had previously received from the Ford Foundation. They no longer needed the Ford Foundation. They had become more independent.

You don't have to be a giant or make large grants to help people or organizations become more independent. In fact, it is easier for a smaller grantmaker to be a catalyst. For example, a scholarship or mentor can change the course of a young person's life, which will in turn change other lives.

6. Embrace Risk (and Failure)

Foundation grants are risk capital. Allocate some or all of these grants to new organizations and ideas. You are free. You are independent from the marketplace and public approval. Failure and criticism will not harm you.

Take a lesson from Rockefeller's story. RIMR achieved near miraculous results, but it had to permit its scientists to "make perfect fools of themselves." Rockefeller's methods and strategy were thoughtful and grounded in experience and knowledge. This gave him the fortitude to follow an unfamiliar path.

New ideas and methods will require foundations to be different, to go against the grain of conventional thinking. Foundation independence permits this. Setbacks and failures are a necessary part of innovation. Have the courage to be honest with yourself and transparent with the world.

This is a cultural issue for foundations. They must consciously create a culture that embraces risk and develop policies to reward bravery and innovation. Leaders must show humility and openness about their own mistakes and imperfections. This will give everyone the courage to speak up and advance new ideas.

Risk is not the same thing as recklessness. Knowledge, experience, and strategy will inspire risk taking. Recklessness is born of ignorance and impulse. Know and practice the difference.

7. Grantmaking to Solve Difficult Problems Requires Perseverance (and Resources)

Helping American high schools to improve graduation rates is more difficult than helping higher education endowments to achieve better investment returns. It is a much more complex problem with many more variables and potential solutions. It follows that measuring the effectiveness of ambitious grants will be more difficult, perhaps impossible, at least in the short to medium term. Did The Gates Foundation's Small Schools initiative fail to improve graduation rates? It seemed so in 2009. Studies years later tend to show that small schools did succeed, at least in New York and Chicago.

Trying to help people solve seemingly intractable problems is a high calling for a grantmaker. Both grantmaker and grantee must grope their way along with all the self-doubt that this entails. Grantmakers must be patient and accept small victories. There is usually no silver bullet. Slow progress is better than what preceded it (nothing). And if grantmakers won't do it, who else can or will? Be intrepid. Persist even in the absence of clear results.

8. Beware of Unintended and Unwanted Consequences

Grantmakers should respect the power of money and not wave it around like a magic wand. A common consequence of careless grantmaking is to influence people and organizations to leave valuable work so that they can follow the money, usually a grantmaker's whim. However, as we have seen from the story of Admiral Peary and Minik, the harm from careless grantmaking can be much worse than wasted time and money.

The best insurance against unintended consequences is a good knowledge of, and an honest relationship with, your grantee partner. JSF has learned to have respect for the power of money and to not lead with it. Diligent inquiry, a thorough understanding of a potential grantee partner, and alignment of interest must come first. In cases in which interests are well aligned, unintended consequences are often positive. For example, in many of the grantor and grantee stories in this chapter, the results were astounding and must have surpassed even the most optimistic expectations.

9. Devise and Follow a Strategy

These stories illustrate the importance of strategy. Carnegie's single-minded focus on the business of creating free libraries allowed him to achieve astonishing results in a relatively short time. The Ford Foundation followed its strategy of grantmaking for the benefit of higher education, which led to one of its most impressive series of grants. Note how its strategy evolved. The Ford Foundation moved from making grants to fund institutional endowments to making grants to help those institutions to earn higher financial returns. Rockefeller's strategy evolved from supporting universities and medical schools to making grants to establish and support the first biomedical research center in the United States.

The most interesting example of the importance of strategy is the Dorr Foundation. It was established to support scientific work in the fields of chemistry and metallurgy. Its principal, John Dorr, became interested in highway safety and simply changed the foundation's strategy. As a small foundation, it was able to act more nimbly and quickly than its larger counterparts. The new strategy was narrow and focused, and the Dorr Foundation followed it until outside lines on highways gained universal acceptance.

10. Make Good Use of Your Foundation's Freedom and Independence

Choose thoughtful, independent grantmaking over self-deluded bliss. Use your freedom to tackle difficult problems that others cannot or will not. Rockefeller's use of philanthropic freedom is a textbook example. Governments could never have taken the political risk of what was then a novel and doubtful enterprise. Once the efficacy of a solution has been proven, governments are able to step in. Smaller foundations and individual grantmakers are even better positioned to break new ground, and we should all invest some of our grant budget in organizations that do innovative work.

The opportunities, large and small, are boundless, and they are out there waiting for you. Use your freedom to find and pursue them.

3

Principles of Foundation Investing

This chapter outlines the theory and principles of foundation investing and why it is vital for foundation leaders to lead the investment process. Like the two previous chapters, its subject matter is conceptual and can be understood without further context. The practical (how to) aspects of leading your foundation's investment require an understanding of how your foundation will govern itself, what vision it has for its grantmaking and how it will fulfill that vision. Therefore, the "how to" discussion appears later, in Chapter 8.

Investing is one of the foundation's two basic operations. Yet it receives much less attention than grantmaking. If you are not an expert investor, you could be forgiven for thinking that the best you can do is hire high-quality investment professionals and leave it to them. However, foundation leaders should involve themselves and lead the investment process, for the following reasons:

1. Investment policy decisions are the biggest driver of investment returns. You, as a foundation leader—not the investment professionals—are best positioned to make and execute those policy decisions.

2. Investing is too important to delegate. Superior returns enable more grantmaking and assure a foundation's future.

3. You don't need to be an expert investor. Leading the investment process is not the same as doing the investing.

Speaking personally to the last point, investing was not part of my pre-foundation background. I am not an expert and do not invest my own money. However, I have learned how to be a leader of a foundation investment process, and JSF's performance is in the top quartile among its peers.[93] The skills and knowledge required to lead the foundation investment process are different from professional investing and not particularly complicated. You can learn and practice them and thereby add value to the foundation's investment process. As you gain more experience and knowledge, your foundation investment practice will improve, and you will add even more value.

SUSTAINABLE INVESTMENT RETURNS

Foundations in the United States and Canada are required to distribute 5 percent of their endowment each year.[94] This minimum required distribution includes grant-related expenses such as salaries for program staff, expenses to investigate grants, and expenses for meetings to discuss grants. It does not include investment and administrative expenses unrelated to grants, which are in addition to the 5 percent minimum required distribution. This means that the minimum spending for a foundation with reasonable investment and administrative expenses will be about 5.3 percent of its endowment each year. Your foundation might be slightly different, but I will use 5.3 percent for the purpose of this discussion.

Based on the above, grantmaking foundations that do not raise money need a real (after inflation) annual investment return of 5.3 percent to sustain themselves. To calculate this, we must add a number for inflation to the foundation's annual investment returns. Over the past one hundred years, inflation has averaged roughly 3 percent per year. This includes double-digit inflation in the seventies and eighties and deflation in the thirties. For the purpose of this discussion, I will assume that inflation will continue to average 3 percent. Thus, a sustainable return is 5.3 percent for annual distributions plus 3 percent for inflation for a total of 8.3 percent.

Some foundations raise money annually or require steady cash flow to support grantee institutions. For these foundations, sustainable returns may not be the primary consideration. However, foundations that do not raise money and aspire to be perpetual (most of them) must average sustainable returns to retain their purchasing power and stay in business. The math is inexorable. If your foundation's annual return is consistently below 8.3 percent then its purchasing power shrinks and eventually disappears. Conversely, if its average investment returns exceed 8.3 percent per year, then it grows its endowment and purchasing power.

I cannot overstate the importance of sustainable investment returns for perpetual foundations. Unfortunately, most fail to achieve them.

THE POWER OF COMPOUND INVESTMENT RETURNS

Over time, the growth of compound investment returns astonishes most people. The results of seemingly trivial differences in annual performance are enormous. I illustrate this with Graph 3.1. It shows three lines that all start with $1 million in 1972 and end in 2022. The graph refers to the Consumer Price Index (CPI), which is a measure of the change over time in the prices paid by consumers for consumer goods and services. The CPI is used to measure inflation and is often used informally as a synonym for inflation.

Assume your foundation starts with $1 million in 1972. If it disburses 5.3 percent per year and averages a sustainable investment return (5.3 percent plus 3 percent for inflation), then it will have $6.7 million in 2022. In real (after inflation) terms the foundation has sustained itself. This is the middle line of Graph 3.1

Now assume that your foundation falls short of a sustainable return by just 1 percent per year. The result of this "small" underperformance is an endowment of less than $4 million, which is worth $608,000 in 1972 dollars. It has lost almost 40 percent of its purchasing power. This is the bottom line of Graph 3.1.

Now assume that your foundation exceeds its sustainable return by an average of 1 percent per year. In 2022 it has over $11 million, which is worth $1.59 million in 1972 dollars. A seemingly small 1 percent annual overperformance has resulted in an increase in its endowment of over 50 percent! This is the top line of Graph 3.1.

The arithmetic demonstrates, better than anything that I can say, the power of compound returns over the sweep of time. What appear to be small differences in performance have massive consequences.

Graph 3.1 Growth of $1 Million from 1972 at CPI -1%, CPI, and CPI +1%, Annualized

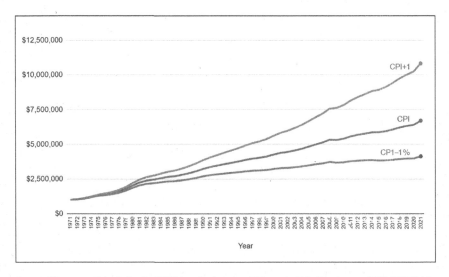

Source: "Consumer Price Index for All Urban Consumers: All Items in U.S. City Average [CPIAUCSL]," FRED, Federal Reserve Bank of St. Louis, U.S. Bureau of Labor Statistics, accessed October 18, 2022, https://fred.stlouisfed.org/series/CPIAUCSL. Past performance is not a guarantee of future results.

THE IMPORTANCE OF ASSET ALLOCATION

The key to achieving sustainable returns is not shrewd stock picking but how a foundation allocates its assets. I will say it again: the biggest driver of investment returns is asset allocation, not stock picking.

Asset allocation means the way a foundation chooses to invest its endowment. It can invest in public stocks, government or corporate bonds, private companies, commodities, a combination of these, and so on. These are called asset classes. A common asset class is stock in public companies or public equity. Over the last one hundred years, public equity has been the path to sustainable returns.

Some foundation leaders balk at owning too much public equity because of risk. Stocks go down in value, sometimes by a lot. However, the long-term performance of the stock market is positive and much better than bonds or any other asset class.

The idea that stocks produce the best long-term returns is neither original nor controversial. There are no guarantees anywhere in life, but if you believe that our society (and the economic system on which it is based) will continue, then there is every reason to suppose that stocks will continue to appreciate. For a persuasive elucidation of this idea, I recommend *Stocks for the Long Run*[95] by Jeremy Siegel, which explains the financial markets with theory and detail that are beyond the scope of this book. I heard Professor Siegel speak at an investment conference about twenty-five years ago, and his investing ideas still underpin much of my understanding of this area.

Consider a hypothetical investment of $100 in stocks in the S&P 500 in 1928, the year before the crash. By the end of 2021, it would have grown to $762,000. In real (after inflation) terms, the $100 has grown to $47,000.

Let's take that same $100 in 1928 and invest in US Treasury bonds. By the end of 2021, it has grown to $9,000 or $530 in 1928 dollars. A $100 investment in corporate bonds would have grown to $47,000 or $3,000 in 1922 dollars.

The difference in the returns of these asset classes bears repeating. In real terms (inflation-adjusted 1928 dollars), the $100 invested in stocks grew to $47,000, the $100 invested in corporate bonds grew to $3,000, and the $100 invested in Treasury bonds grew to $530. Bonds, government or corporate, didn't come close to producing a sustainable investment return for a grantmaking foundation. For foundation investors, the real risk is not a precipitous drop in value of the portfolio. The real risk is failing to achieve sustainable investment returns over the long term.

I am not suggesting that foundations should not own bonds. Bonds are necessary to provide liquidity for grantmaking. Foundations must balance their need for liquidity against their need for sustainable returns. This is the art of asset allocation policy, and it should be tailored to the needs of your unique foundation.

This is good news for foundation leaders. Unlike the financial markets, asset allocation is completely within their control. If foundation leaders get this right, then they are well on their way to sustainable returns.

VOLATILITY AND RISK

You might reasonably ask, "If successful investing is as simple as making the right asset allocation policy, then why doesn't everybody do it?" The answer is that superior long-term investment returns are accompanied by drama, in the form of volatility. Volatility is the propensity of public equity values to unpredictably change. The crashes of 1929, 1973–4, and 2008–9 are burned into the consciousness of investors. How can you trust an investment class that loses half of its value in a few months?

Investors must look past fluctuations in price and focus on the inherent value of the shares that they own. Panic selling may drive prices down quickly, but history has shown that investors who held fast and did not sell during these downturns lost nothing. Their stocks rebounded and went on to earn large returns. The volatility of equity investments is like a roller coaster. If investors do not get off when the roller coaster goes down, there is little risk. People who think that there is more inherent risk in owning stocks instead of bonds are confusing risk with volatility.

The alternative to the volatility of stocks is a "safe" mix of a smaller public equity allocation, more bonds, and maybe some other diversified assets that are less correlated to the stock market. This will give your foundation a more comfortable ride, but it comes at the expense of long-term investment performance. For foundations that aspire to perpetuity, the real risk is low investment returns. There is no safety in playing it safe.

Just because volatility is not risky over the long term doesn't mean that there is no risk in the public equity markets. There are plenty of ways for a foundation to lose its money. Concentrating investments in too few companies, even sound ones, is an example of risk. If one or more of these companies fail, you will lose money that cannot be recovered. When I say that stocks appreciate over the long term, I am referring to the broad market. The fortunes of individual companies (and their stocks) wax and wane. However, these average out and the market, as a whole, appreciates over the long term.

Another example of risk is to buy stock at a very high price. How do you know when a stock is trading at a "very high price"? The price of a share is measured as a multiple of its earnings, called the price/earnings (P/E) ratio. If a stock earns one dollar a share and sells for fifteen dollars a share, then its P/E ratio is fifteen. Some stocks and industries have higher P/E ratios than others but the historical average P/E ratio for the S&P 500 or the S&P/TSX composite is about seventeen. Faster growing companies generally have higher P/E ratios.

Over the last fifty years P/E ratios have mostly ranged from the single digits to the forties. The usual range is from the high teens to the high twenties. When investors feel exuberant, average P/E ratios increase and when they are pessimistic, P/E ratios decline.

In the late 1990s, investors bought technology companies in the NASDAQ index at prices of 150 times earnings or more. They were infatuated with tech stocks and the Internet and lost their sense of value. Prices eventually reverted to historical norms and the NASDAQ index crashed and did not rebound. Even today it trades at about half of what it did over twenty years ago. Investors who paid those high prices lost money. Many investors in the Nikkei market in the 1980s paid extraordinarily high prices for stocks. The story is similar. Investors were infatuated with Japan's business prowess and lost their sense of value (and their money).

As I write, shares of Tesla are trading at over 200 times earnings and Amazon is trading at over 100 times earnings. Investors buying at these prices are taking a risk. They have done very well so far, but if market sentiment changes, many of them will lose money. Conversely, a share of one of my favorite banks can be bought for seven times earnings. Banks tend to have lower P/E ratios but even allowing for this, a P/E ratio of seven is the equivalent of a half-price sale. Yet investor sentiment is negative. Volatility is scary. Risk is dangerous.

DISCLAIMER

Investment pitches are always accompanied by a disclaimer, the gist of which is that "past performance is not a guarantee of future performance." As a warning this statement is a dismal failure. Of course, past performance is not a guarantee. Investors already know that. What they want to know is whether past performance likely foretells future performance. The reversion to the mean theory says that it doesn't. It says that if an investment is performing exceptionally well (or poorly) then it will correct and return to average. But when?

The following advice from American humorist Will Rogers may be more useful: "Take all your savings and buy some good stock and hold it till it goes up, then sell it. If it don't go up, don't buy it."

Rogers puts his finger on the investor's impossible predicament. Investment strategies are based upon experience, but investment performance depends on what happens in the future.

THE BEHAVIOR GAP

The emotional component of volatility deserves more discussion. Investors feel greed when the market is up and fear when it is down. Fear seems to be the dominant emotion. Nobel laureate Daniel Kahneman, in *Thinking, Fast and Slow*,[96] describes how human evolution and survival have taught us to give greater weight to a potential adverse result than a positive one. This is reflected in investor behavior. People tend to be more afraid of losing and this causes them to sell after small market downturns and miss out when the market rebounds to higher levels. The result is poor investor returns, even when the investment itself has done well. Carl Richards calls this the *behavior gap*, the difference between what an investment earns and what an average investor gets:

> When the market soars or hits a rough patch, there's a natural tendency to do something. Fast. Our natural reaction is to sell after bad news (when the market is already down) and buy when news is good (after the market is already up), thus indulging our fear and our greed. It's an impossible strategy.[97]

Graph 3.2 Twenty-Year Average Annual Returns (2002–21) versus
Investor Behavior

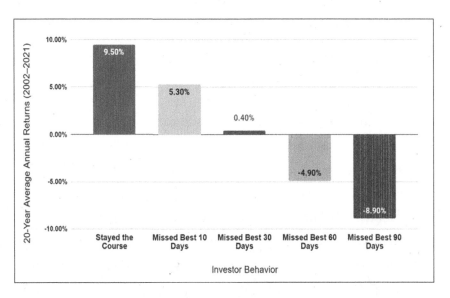

Source: Davis Advisors, "Timeless Wisdom for Creating Long-Term Wealth," Davis Funds, December 2022, https://davisfunds.com/downloads/TW.pdf. The market is represented by the S&P 500 Index. Investments cannot be made directly in an Index. Past performance is not a guarantee of future results.

Graph 3.2 illustrates Richards's point.

Between 2002 and 2021, the S&P 500 returned 9.5 percent annually, as shown by the bar, and this is what you would have earned
had you ignored the downturns and simply held the investment. Had
you been out of the market for its best ten days, your return would
have been cut almost in half. Just ten days over twenty years! Had
you missed the ninety best days of these twenty years, you would
have lost 8.9 percent annually, almost all your money! You might
say that if you had missed the worst ninety days instead of the best
then you would have done even better than the index. That is true,
except that it doesn't usually work that way. Poor investors tend to
sell after a downturn and get back in after the market has gone up.

The behavior gap causes them to earn lower returns. The remedy is to understand and resist the emotional pull of our instinctive fear and greed.

REPUTATIONAL RISK

If your foundation is sufficiently sophisticated to overcome the behavior gap, there is another problem that is not emotional, but rational. It causes most investment managers to underperform the index, most advisers to recommend asset allocations that underperform, and most foundations to fail in their quest for sustainable returns. This problem is reputational risk, and it goes like this. Everyone agrees on the importance of long-term returns, but the people who are supposed to achieve them are judged in the short term. Their reputations are damaged by the inevitable short-term reverses of pursuing a long-term strategy.

Reputational risk causes investment advisers and fund managers to avoid volatility. They would prefer higher investment returns, but their overriding interest is to retain their clients. They know that they are less likely to get fired if their clients' asset values do not drop precipitously and are in step with their peers'.

Fund managers know that the true value of out-of-favor companies will eventually be recognized by the market. But when? Nobody, including the manager, has the slightest idea. The manager does know, however, that the result of going against market sentiment may be significant underperformance over one, three, or even five years. This is enough time for the manager to lose most of its business, and by then, being right hardly matters. The problem for everybody—investment advisers, managers, and even foundation leaders—is the reputational risk posed by a long-term strategy.

I have said that foundation leaders are best positioned to formulate and execute investment policy. This is because the antidote for both reputational risk and emotional barriers is in the hands of foundation leaders only. They can pursue a long-term strategy and accept the volatility that goes with it. This means putting the foundation's interests ahead of their personal interest in being comfortable or appearing to be right. Only they can build the political will to pursue an investment policy that will produce sustainable returns over time. Only foundation leaders can convince their advisers that they will not judge by short-term results but by the quality of the plan and the ability to execute. Everyone's eyes will naturally be drawn to recent performance, but foundation leaders can make it clear by their talk and actions that this does not govern their decisions.

JSF employed an investment manager that went through a four-year period of underperforming its peers and the index by about 3 percent, which placed it in the bottom quartile of its peers. The manager noted that its investment style was out of favor with market sentiment and pointed out that the intrinsic value of the companies in its portfolio had continued to rise. The manager was confident that this would eventually be recognized by the market and the prices of these companies would increase. There had been no significant change in the manager's key personnel or investing style. We didn't like the underperformance, but we had faith in the manager and the explanation made sense. In 2020 the manager outperformed the market and its peers and did so again in 2021 and overall has been a top quartile investor for the foundation. Does this mean that JSF should keep this manager forever? No. Someday, inevitably, this manager will change its people and its investing style and revert to the mean, and JSF, if it is doing its job properly, will replace it.

The essential task for foundation leaders is to focus on a long-term strategy and to convince their investment advisers to do likewise. Brilliance is not required but leadership is essential.

OTHER THINGS YOU SHOULD KNOW

The following subjects will likely be relevant to your investment practice. The list is not definitive, any more than this chapter is a definitive treatise on investing. This object is not to teach you everything that you need to know about investing but to get you started in the right direction. Your foundation investment practice will improve as you acquire more knowledge and experience.

Index Funds and Exchange-Traded Funds

Index funds and exchange-traded funds (ETFs) are funds that hold stocks or bonds in exact proportion to a particular index. For example, an index fund based upon the S&P 500 will own shares in the companies that compose the S&P 500 in exact proportion to their weight in that index. The S&P TSX index is a composite of 250 stocks on the Toronto Stock Exchange. There is a public equity index for most developed countries and for emerging and frontier markets. The advantages of index funds are twofold. First, they give broad market exposure. When I said earlier that public equity returns are superior to bonds, I was using returns of the S&P 500 index. For the foundation investor, ETFs have the same characteristics as index funds and I do not differentiate; the discussion of index funds applies to ETFs with equal force.

The second advantage of index funds is low fees. Buying and selling within these funds is done according to their weighting within the index. It is a purely mechanical process with no subjective input. There are no analysts or portfolio managers to pay. A typical managed fund charges an annual fee of 1 percent of the assets it manages. Most index funds cost less than one-tenth of that. Savings on fees go right to your foundation's bottom line and compound annually. If the savings seem small or insignificant, review the section on compound investment returns and calculate the difference to your foundation's endowment over time.

I have already noted that most fund managers underperform the index. If index funds are cheaper and usually outperform active fund managers, why doesn't everyone own index funds? The answer is that most of them should.

Warren Buffett observed in his 2017[98] letter to investors that most investors would be better off buying index funds. Another investing giant of our era, the recently deceased John Bogle, wrote *The Little Book of Common Sense Investing*,[99] which explains the theory behind index funds and their efficacy. It is an entertaining read, which will enhance your understanding of the financial markets. I can only add that if your foundation is paying fees to managers who underperform the index, then it will be very difficult for it to achieve sustainable investment returns.

JSF's experience supports the case for index funds. Over the past twenty-five years we have found only two public equity managers who have significantly outperformed the index over the long term. Together they invest 25 percent of JSF's endowment, and without them JSF would not be a top quartile investor.[100]

I do not offer JSF's experience with investment managers as a ringing endorsement of active investment management. The choice between active managers and index funds is different for each foundation. Do you have the capacity to look for exceptional managers and monitor them? Do you have the time and the interest?

Apologists for managed funds point out that most of them do better than index funds at times when the market is going down. This is true and, for foundations that need steady cash flow, it may be worth the penalty in performance. However, for most foundations, the object of investing is not to do better in down markets but to do better over the long term. In the absence of extraordinary investment managers, index funds have been the surest way to do better over the long term. Historically, most market indices have produced sustainable returns over the long term. Foundations with their assets in either the S&P 500, S&P TSX composite, or MSCI EAFE indices over the last hundred years would have outperformed their peers and enjoyed sustainable returns.

Private Equity and Venture Capital Funds

Private equity and venture capital funds are usually in the form of partnerships, where investors are limited partners and the firm running the fund is the general partner. Larger foundations and institutional endowments are ideal investors because of their ability to commit large sums (upward of $1 million) for long periods of time, usually ten years or more. The foundation's financial commitment is called when the general partner needs it to buy something and returned when the general partner has sold something. There is no right to sell or refuse a cash call, regardless of performance. The only way out is to find a secondary buyer who will take the investment off your hands for a distressed price.

Private and venture capital fund fees are outlandishly high. Typically, they charge a base fee of 1 to 2 percent on committed capital plus

20 percent of profits in excess of 6 or 8 percent. These fees do not relate to the costs of running the funds as much as the value that they are supposed to add. In 2021, for example, JSF's allocation to private equity/venture capital returned over 50 percent. Some of its managers had funds of several billion dollars. Imagine the fees generated for those managers on returns of 50 percent!

The high fees and illiquidity of these funds only make sense when returns are significantly above market. Unfortunately, most private equity/venture capital funds do not perform much better than the index of publicly traded stocks. However, a few managers have funds that are consistently in the top quartile, and these are the ones your foundation must own. An investment adviser who can help a foundation gain access to first quartile private equity and venture capital managers performs a great service. Your adviser may also recommend *funds of funds*, which are bundled parts of eight or ten different private equity or venture capital funds. In addition to diversification, this helps investors, particularly small ones, to gain access to the top funds. However, it adds another layer of fees to what is already an expensive product.

Hedge Funds

What is a hedge fund? Is it a different asset class? Is it an investment style? Hedge funds differ greatly and employ a wide range of strategies, but their distinguishing characteristic is usually fees. A typical hedge fund charges 1 or 2 percent of assets under management plus 20 percent of annual profits. One would think that anyone charging a fee that large would produce high returns. Hedge funds, however, are legendary underperformers.

In 2005, Warren Buffett publicly offered to bet $500,000 (all proceeds to charity) that no investment professional could select a set of at least five hedge funds that would match the returns of an index fund based upon the S&P 500 over a period of ten years. One investor, a co-manager of Protege Partners, LLC, took him up on it. After ten years, the hedge funds had returned an average annual return of 2.2 percent per year versus the S&P 500 return of 7.1 percent. That means $1 million invested in the hedge funds would have gained $220,000 and the index fund would have gained $854,000.[101]

Why would anyone buy hedge funds? Their supporters—a surprising number—cite their defensive value. Most hedge funds are less correlated with the market and tend to perform better when the market goes down. For long-term investors, the defensive value of hedge funds seems overstated. Investors who expected hedge funds to provide liquidity during the market crisis of 2008–9 would have been disappointed. Unlike bonds, most of them had grossly lower valuations and/or restrictions to prevent investors from getting at their money. Hedge funds do dampen volatility, but for the long-term investor, the object is to make money, not dampen volatility.

Hedge funds might have a place for foundations that require steadier investment returns. However, for foundations that need sustainable returns, the logic of investing in a hedge fund seems flawed. The long-term investor hitches its wagon to the market and hopes that it will continue to grow wealth. Why bet against the market? If the financial markets fail, a small hedge fund allocation won't save the foundation. And if the markets continue to do what they have done in the past, then a hedge fund will be a drag on performance.

Commodities, Energy, and Real Estate

Runaway inflation is the investor's worst nightmare, and many foundations hedge against inflation by owning assets such as commodities, energy, and real estate that will increase in price with inflation. The problem with these assets is that they underperform equity during noninflationary periods. Stock prices also increase with inflation, albeit not as quickly, because share earnings adjust to inflation. A large allocation to good-quality equity investments serves as an inflation hedge and is more productive than real estate, commodities, and energy.

Environmental, Social, and Governance

Environmental, social, and governance (ESG)[102] is not "woke capitalism" or a passing fad. It has been a quiet revolution among investors and public companies around the world. Ten years ago, most foundation investment committees took the position that their job was to make money. Unless an investment was contrary to mission (for example, investment in a coal mine by an environmentally focused foundation), most committees took little interest in how returns were generated. Today a foundation with that attitude would be failing in its fiduciary duty. ESG is here to stay, and foundation leaders need to understand it.

In 2006, two United Nations (UN) agencies created the Principles for Responsible Investment (PRI). This declaration has created a UN-supported network of investment managers that in total manage over $90 trillion in assets. This represents 80 percent of the professionally managed capital in the world. The PRI redefines fiduciary duty for the twenty-first century: "Fiduciary duty [now] . . . requires investors to incorporate all value drivers, including environmental, social, and governance factors, in investment decision making."[103] The focus of investors must now be on the long term and consider the environment and society.

The PRI has developed a reporting module for money managers, who use it to report annually and are given a letter grade. Not only does a foundation know whether a manager is a PRI signatory, but it can now see how its performance has been graded. At JSF, we have focused on two main aspects of ESG: integration and active ownership. Integration means that a money manager must demonstrate that its investment process considers long-term ESG risks and opportunities. Active ownership means that the manager must engage companies on ESG issues and support its positions with strategic proxy voting.

Within the last few years, ESG has worked its way into the mainstream of foundation investing. It is a major triumph for long-term investors and is a welcome story in a time when governments do not face global issues with a harmonious worldview. It is also an example of the power of the private non-governmental organizations, of which foundations form a large part.

THE REWARDS OF INDEPENDENCE

I recount the story of Theodore and Vivian Johnson, who were JSF's founders. I do not recommend their approach to foundation investors. Their investment advisers would not think it wise, and they would be acting contrary to their fiduciary duty to the foundation. The story is nonetheless interesting and instructive.

In 1920, a young Theodore Johnson responded to a newspaper ad for employment with a small company in Los Angeles, the Merchants

Parcel Delivery. In those days, merchants provided home delivery of goods purchased in-store by their customers. The Merchants Parcel Delivery could deliver the parcels more efficiently than individual merchants, and it quickly established a good local business. Mr. Johnson became one of about three hundred employees. He had a university degree in business (unusual for the time) and went to night school and obtained a master's degree. He became vice president of what was then called industrial relations. By then, the company had renamed itself United Parcel Service (UPS).

By today's standards, Mr. Johnson was modestly paid; he never earned a salary of more than $17,000 per year. But as a member of senior management, he was permitted to buy stock in UPS, which was still privately owned. He bought as much stock as he reasonably could, at every opportunity. Mr. Johnson thought that the company's stock was conservatively valued and would appreciate. When he retired in 1951, he and Mrs. Johnson had accumulated about $700,000 (about $7.5 million in today's dollars). This was enough for a comfortable retirement, but they could hardly be described as rich. Most of their wealth was in UPS shares. They kept their shares and did not diversify.

Mr. and Mrs. Johnson's act of keeping their UPS shares was an act of risk, a bet on the fortunes of one company. If UPS failed, they would lose their money. The Johnsons knew that. They also knew that UPS was a profitable, well-run company in an expanding business. They knew that it was much more likely that UPS would prosper, and the value of its shares would continue to appreciate.

Mr. and Mrs. Johnson's bet on UPS was a good one. However, it did not accord with conventional investment practice. Their advisers counselled them to diversify. Had they done so, they would have been unable to make most of their philanthropic gifts during their lives and would not have had money to endow JSF.

As it turned out, the Johnsons' UPS shares were worth more than $60 million by the late 1980s, even after their significant charitable gifts. In the 1990s, JSF continued to hold most of its UPS stock. In 1999 UPS went public and the value of JSF's endowment nearly doubled.

The Johnsons and JSF had what Peter Lynch would have called an edge.[104] Mr. Johnson knew UPS well and had the right to buy its shares. When he retired, he continued to follow and understand UPS, as did his son Ted after Mr. Johnson's death. Once UPS became a public company, the edge was lost. Everyone had access to the company's information and the playing field was levelled.

PRINCIPLES OF FOUNDATION INVESTING

These principles are culled from the preceding discussion and can serve as a summary or reminder of the main points made.

1. Foundation leaders, and not the experts, are in the best position to add value to foundation investment returns and should therefore lead the foundation's investment process.

2. Formulating and executing an investment policy are a foundation's most important investment actions and should be led by foundation leaders, who best know their foundation's unique character and needs. This requires foundation leaders to familiarize themselves with the basic

concepts of investing. The heart of investment policy is asset allocation, which governs how the foundation allocates its endowment to the financial markets. Asset allocation, not stock picking, accounts for most of the foundation's investment performance.

3. Seemingly insignificant differences in investment returns can mean the difference between foundation growth and extinction. Be aware of the power of compound returns over long periods of time.

4. Foundations that do not have fixed grantee obligations and intend to exist for thirty years or more should strive for sustainable returns. These are investment returns that equal the foundation's charitable distributions and non-grant expenses of about 5.3 percent plus inflation, which has averaged about 3 percent annually over the last one hundred years. In nominal terms this means an annual investment return of 8.3 percent net of fees, which is difficult to achieve. The real hazard for most foundations is inferior investment returns over the long term, not a market crash. Foundations can recover from the latter but not the former. Foundations must distinguish between the roller coaster aspect of the equity markets (volatility) and the risk of irretrievably losing money.

5. Volatility is the inevitable rise and fall of stock prices in response to events and market sentiment. It is important to remember that historically the long-term trend

has been upward. For long-term investors, volatility is unpleasant but not particularly dangerous. The greater risk lies in selling your stock when the market is down and missing the recovery. Other risky strategies include concentrating your portfolio on one or a few companies and paying excessive prices for stocks.

6. It is a truism that you can't time the market, although many investors try. Humans are emotionally inclined to buy when stocks are going up and sell when they are going down, which is a losing strategy. The nimble savant who quickly darts in and out of the market is a myth. Nobody knows when the market will rise or fall. Foundation leaders must remind themselves that stock prices are driven by market sentiment (which defies logic) and future events (which cannot be predicted).

   Reversion to the mean is a useful theory to help us curb our instinct to chase winners and dump losers. The theory postulates that when stock prices are out of line with historical averages (either high or low), they will eventually revert to the mean. Another way to say this: prices will correct. This theory will not help you to time the market, however, because it cannot predict when prices will correct.

7. Reputational risk causes most investment advisers, money managers, and foundations to fear short-term losses, and this causes them to prefer defensive, diversified portfolios that underperform in the long term. This issue should be recognized and honestly discussed with the foundation's

board and investment professionals. If the foundation's goal is sustainable long-term performance, then its asset allocation policy should reflect that goal and foundation leaders must build the political will to follow policy in the face of volatility.

8. Most active money managers who invest in public equities underperform the index over the long term. In the absence of extraordinary managers, a foundation is better off with index funds, which offer lower fees and better performance.

9. Unless your foundation's circumstances require it, avoid or limit diversification strategies that hedge market risk. It is difficult to achieve sustainable returns when you bet against the market (and pay high fees).

10. Private capital and venture capital partnerships are asset classes that have become popular with larger foundations over the past thirty years. The best of these funds produce net returns well above market indices and can significantly improve investment performance. However, there is a wide dispersion between the best funds and those funds in the third and fourth quartile. Unless you can obtain access to top funds, do not invest in these asset classes. These funds, especially venture capital, have relatively high risk and high fees, and require large financial commitments over long periods of time.

11. Investing rewards independence and risk taking. Do not confuse a calculated risk with rash behavior, however.

12. And this above all else. Investing, like everything else, involves risk and there is no guarantee that the financial markets will continue to produce gains for long-term investors. "Uncertainty is the only certainty there is and knowing how to live with insecurity is the only security."[105]

4

Foundation Governance

Regardless of the size of your foundation or whether it has staff, good governance is the elixir that makes everything work. If your foundation is well governed, it will eventually be a good grantmaker and investor. This chapter discusses the principles and practices of good foundation governance.

Before continuing, I make two disclaimers. First, there are volumes of good literature on board governance and successful organizations, which I do not intend to synthesize. Two books I recommend are *Built to Last*[106] and *Governance as Leadership*.[107] Building and maintaining an excellent organization and effective leadership are not always intuitive, and it is useful for the board and senior staff to read, discuss, and follow the teachings of a good book. In this book, I deal only with board and organizational aspects as they seem particularly relevant to foundations. Second, I cite and rely extensively on examples of JSF's governance. These are not intended to show the right way (there is no right way) or even best practice. They simply illustrate a way of doing things that has worked for us. You will know if it works for your foundation and, if not, how to change or modify it so that it does.

THE BOARD OF DIRECTORS

The quality of a foundation is determined by the quality of its board. Recruiting and maintaining high-quality directors is a prerequisite to a great board. You need to have the right people on the bus. The board should be knowledgeable of the foundation's business, curious, diligent, and respectful. Collectively, it should be wiser and smarter than any of the individuals that comprise it.

The imperative of a good board is the same in a large foundation, run by a chief executive, as it is in a small foundation where there are few or no staff. In some foundations, a strong CEO, with influence regarding board recruitment, may help a foundation to develop a good board. In foundations without staff, this CEO role may be vested in the board chair or another key board member. For many foundations, the primary responsibility for board recruitment falls to a governance committee.

A good board sets the tone for a strong organizational culture, where leaders and staff put the interests of the foundation first in everything they do. Everyone feels respected and valued and, in this environment, everyone is free to give their best effort. A robust culture permeates everything that a foundation does. How is such a culture built?

FAMILY DYNAMICS

For boards with several family members, a healthy board culture is especially important. Such a culture is built around a shared ethic that the interests of the foundation are paramount, and those interests are defined by the board and not individual board members. Board members respect the foundation's mission, other board members, and the governance process. Humility and objectivity are the answer to family dynamics, even complicated ones!

A good board must be engaged, not managed. At meetings, this means encouraging diverse views, dissent, and debate. Board members should not be inhibited by a need to conform and should feel free to be honest and say what they are thinking. Disagreement and dissent will make good ideas clearer and expose bad ones. Ideas are judged by their merits and not by the status of the people who hold them. Board members trust each other and do not assume that those who disagree with them are wrong. Instead, they probe for further information. They ask, "Why?" "How do you know that?" They are open to being persuaded by new information and perspectives.

Goodwill and humility are hallmarks of excellent boards. This does not mean "groupthink" or going along to please others, which can cause your board to make terrible decisions that nobody wants. The "Abilene Paradox"[108] vividly illustrates the perils of suppressing your own opinion to accommodate others. Board debate should be vigorous, lively, and honest. Consensus is not always possible. The key is a good process in which every board member feels that they have been heard. Once a decision has been made, there is no place for revisiting it, complaining about it, or reminding the board that "I told you so."

Some observers think that good organizations are propelled by gifted and charismatic leaders, with a supporting cast in tow. The opposite is usually true. To borrow an analogy, a good organization is like a well-built clock.[109] It is the entire organization that propels the foundation. The leader is an integral part of the organization, but the leader's main job is to look after the clock, not to be brilliant and charismatic. Once an organization's leader assumes a rock star persona, it is a sure sign it has lost its way and is headed for mediocrity.

The job of a meeting chair is to get the best from the group and not to obtain the right decision or to have all the bright ideas. If the chair dominates meetings, strong directors and committee members will not be as interested or engaged, and the organization gets less from them. Usually, questions are more important than answers and the chair should subjugate personal views to the group's discussion. Otherwise, the meeting may be influenced by the chair's preference. I have chaired many meetings of JSF's grant committee at which the group arrived at a different position than I would have. On some of those occasions I changed my mind and on others I didn't. I cannot say whether I or the committee had the right answer at the end. However, the quality of the debate was always more important than the answer.

The culture of a board and foundation is also built outside of meetings. JSF's board comes from diverse parts of the United States and Canada. We meet in person three times a year, always in a place where we have grantees. We host a dinner for grantees and potential grantees. This is an important event and partners often attend. On the free nights, board members may go out for dinner together or to a sporting event or concert. Board members and many of their partners have become friends and look forward to seeing each other.[110]

In my view, large boards or frequent meetings do not add value to the work of the foundation. Too many people around the table makes meaningful engagement more difficult. The ideal size for most foundation boards is ten or fewer. Two to four meetings per year should be sufficient for a foundation board; most of the work is done by its committees. JSF has six standing committees (described below) and seven voting board members. Most board members serve on at least three committees.

BOARD AND STAFF PARTNERSHIP

In foundations with staff, the board governs and the staff manages. Basic responsibilities of both are set out in the sidebar. It is essential for board and staff to understand their respective roles, and these should be clearly defined. A common sin of inexperienced board members is a tendency to micromanage, to second-guess staff or encroach on foundation management issues. In my previous career, I advised boards and I used to tell them that "the board sets the course, and the staff sails the ship." This is a simplification, but it is easy to understand and remember. Governance education is usually the remedy to board over-involvement and should be copiously applied.

In foundations with no staff, the board governs and also manages. Some board members must wear more than one hat. In addition to their board duties, they assume operational responsibilities. The same considerations apply, and the partnership is between the whole board and individual board members who have been charged with management and operational functions. The respective roles must be clearly spelled out and the job descriptions adapted accordingly. For example, if the board chair also functions as a CEO or a treasurer also functions as a CFO, they should have corresponding job descriptions for each role. And the rest of the board should respect those job descriptions. In this chapter (and in this book) a reference to staff includes board members who perform staff functions.

In excellent organizations, with a high-functioning partnership between board and staff, their respective roles can be fluid at the margins. In *Governance as Leadership*, the partnership is compared to a doubles team in tennis where play and positioning of the players are influenced by the flow of the game and not determined solely by fixed lines of authority.[111] This is where the CEO and board understand their roles well and do not feel the need to jealously guard their turf. They feel safe to ask for and receive help.

The relationship between board and staff requires mutual trust and respect. The board must value the staff and treat them accordingly. The staff must understand that they are employed by the foundation and therefore by the board. If the staff let themselves believe that the board's purpose is ceremonial and they are the ones really running the organization then they will take liberties, which inevitably leads to disruption and instability.

RESPECTIVE RESPONSIBILITIES OF BOARD AND CEO (STAFF)

Board
- Governs the foundation
- Accountable for foundation's operations and the pursuit of its mission
- Oversees foundation grantmaking, investing, and spending
- Develops policy; receives and disposes committee recommendations
- Hires and supervises the foundation's CEO
- Upholds and promotes the foundation's values; places its best interests above all else

CEO (Staff)

- Manages all aspects of the foundation's operations
- Supports board and committee meetings: in consultation with board and committee chairs, prepares agendas and materials, arranges facilities
- Executes the foundation's mission, strategy, and vision of the future, as approved by the board
- Deals with grantees, investment managers, bankers, consultants, and suppliers
- Internally, CEO acts as the interface between board and staff
- Acts as key spokesperson for the foundation

The contact points for the partnership between board and staff are the board chair and committee chairs and the CEO. The mutual trust and respect between board and staff must manifest itself in these relationships. Trust means more than a belief in the other person's bona fides and goodwill. It extends to belief in the other person's ability and judgment. Board chair and CEO need to listen to each other, disagree occasionally, and find common ground. Mutual trust and respect will make it safe for them to admit mistakes, learn from them, and otherwise allow themselves to be vulnerable. They should be allied in the pursuit of engaging the board. The board chair supervises the CEO, but the CEO's evaluation should be done by the full board, usually once a year. As board chair of JSF, I meet with the CEO once a month with an agenda that we both prepare.

The partnership is obviously in trouble if the CEO thinks that the board is a nuisance to be tolerated and managed or if the CEO is afraid of the board. The CEO's attitude, whatever it is, will find its way into the staff and influence its thinking and behavior. If a board chronically micromanages its CEO, unilaterally reduces the CEO's authority or starts meeting out of the presence of the CEO, then the relationship is untenable. A CEO in that situation must make a stand. The board must change its ways, or the CEO should find another job. A board that does not trust and respect its CEO must either resolve the underlying issue or end the relationship. These are not easy problems and require searching, honest, and fair discussion. If you are a senior leader of an organization that is incapable of this, then you should leave. The inability to talk honestly is a hallmark of a weak organization and an unhealthy culture.

NO-NOS

Here are three things that good board members do not do:

1. **They do not have private meetings outside board meetings.**

   This is a common sin of misdirected board members. They call each other before a meeting to discuss an issue on an upcoming agenda. This detracts from the quality of the meeting, and a good chair will usually sense when an agenda item has been discussed outside the committee or board. Sometimes people will linger in the parking lot after a meeting and say things that they didn't say in the meeting. This is never helpful. The only place for board and committee business is where all are present. The exceptions to this rule are where a subgroup has been legitimately tasked, or the chair is performing its duties.

   I am not suggesting that board members should never talk about foundation business outside meetings. The discussion and exchange of ideas between board members is natural and there is nothing wrong with it, provided it does not undermine a board decision or its discussion of an upcoming agenda item. Board members need self-awareness and thoughtfulness to know when their conduct is subversive. They should conduct themselves as if the entire board were watching and ask themselves if their comments are something that they should or would say in its presence. They must trust the process and leave important business for the board and its committees.

2. **They do not deal independently with the CEO, staff, grantees, or anyone else.**

    A board member calls the CEO or staff member and gives direction or a suggestion. Worse yet, the board member calls a grantee to discuss a grant. A CEO who becomes aware of such behavior should alert the board chair, who must put a stop to it. Board and committee chairs deal with the CEO, and the CEO deals with staff, grantees, and everyone else. The board speaks with one voice and that is through its chair. Board members do not freelance or take it upon themselves to act on behalf of the foundation.

    I emphasize (again) that I do not mean to lay down rigid rules for every situation. Instead of rules, board members need to understand and follow basic principles. For example, it is perfectly acceptable in most organizations for board members to contact staff members on housekeeping matters such as expense reports and the like. Similarly, board members can deal with grantees (any anybody else) if they have been directed to do so.

3. **They do not micromanage.**

   Few things are as demoralizing as board members who want to
   micromanage. A frequent version of this is a board member who
   wants to instruct staff on management issues. Or a CEO or committee chair brings a report to a meeting and, instead of focusing
   on the idea, the board member wants to change a name, a phrase,
   or some other minor point. A good chair will bring the discussion back on track, but the damage has been done, time has been
   wasted, and the meeting suffers. Every board member has the
   right to be wrong or misspeak occasionally. That is part of a free
   and lively exchange. But board members who fail to understand
   their role and repeatedly insist on trivial changes to the work of
   others should be curbed or, better yet, replaced.

FOUNDATION COMMITTEES

In most foundations, committees are where the work of the board is
done and where directors can be engaged to great advantage. Foundation committees typically cover the following areas: grantmaking,
investing, governance and nominating, compensation, audit and risk
management, and executive and financial functions.

Committee work should be fairly spread among the board according to personal interest, talent, and experience. Normally, the board
chair proposes the committee assignments and the board votes. Before
the vote, the chair usually asks if anyone has been saddled with a committee they do not want or has been overlooked for one that they do.

The CEO is often an ex officio member of all committees except
compensation. Committees should have job descriptions, and basic
descriptions of the main functions are inset.

Grant Committee

Grantmaking is a foundation's most meaningful and interesting work and most of your board members will be members of this committee. At JSF, every board member serves on the grant program committee, and it has two outside members. JSF's board has authorized it to make foundation grant decisions. In some foundations the board makes the grant decisions. For those foundations, this discussion applies to the board.

The size of a foundation's grant budget usually determines how its grant committee functions. In larger foundations, the grant committee sets the policy and priorities, and staff make the grants and report to the committee. At the other end of the spectrum, the committees of most small foundations review and decide every grant application. At JSF, the grant committee reviews and decides most grant applications, and this is the process that I will use to illustrate the work of the committee.

JSF's grant committee meets three times per year and the agenda is prepared by the CEO in consultation with the committee chair. Materials are electronically circulated at least one week in advance (ten days is better). We use Diligent Boards software. Meetings typically last about six hours. Potential grantees appear in person or virtually to present an application. Grantees sometimes appear to give a report or an update.

A good grant committee considers the merit of grant applications and how they fit with foundation strategy and does not rubber-stamp staff recommendations. This means that the foundation must reconcile two seemingly opposed ideas: respect for the work and superior knowledge of the staff who developed the grant application and respect for the committee's prerogative to decide. This can only be achieved by engaging the committee at the beginning of the grant process.

The grant committee should see all grant inquiries, including those rejected by staff. Promising ideas should be brought to the committee for discussion and direction. When staff pursue ideas, the committee should be apprised of every step and invited to weigh in. By the time an application makes it to committee, its members should be familiar with and expecting it. The committee's participation along the way will affirm staff's work and reduce the likelihood that staff feel undermined by committee decisions. The process will be adapted, depending upon the size and number of grant applications, but the basic premise is the same: the committee should be involved from the beginning.

The committee's buy-in from the beginning of an idea increases the likelihood that the grant application will be approved. However, the committee should be free to decline an application or send it back for reworking. Sometimes the committee will see something that staff didn't. Maybe it doesn't fit with some aspect of strategy or doesn't work for some other reason. This should not happen often but, when it does, staff should not feel affronted or diminished. On the occasions that it happened when I was CEO, the discussions behind the decision were among the committee's best and usually changed my mind also. It is true: the wisdom of the group is greater than any single person in it.

In addition to deciding grant applications, the committee has a continuing responsibility for developing and recommending grantmaking policy to the board. The committee must constantly question strategy and whether it should be affirmed or modified. Grant outcomes must be held up against theories of change. The committee should obtain information and ideas from grantees, consultants, and other experts. Does the information support our strategy? Why?

The grant committee should participate in other basic aspects of grantmaking, including site visits and convenings. Whether that means participating in the actual events or discussing them within the committee depends upon the foundation's style and volume of work. Either way, meeting with grantees and their communities is the highest form of engagement and one of the committee's most useful and enjoyable activities. Site visits and convenings are managed by the CEO, who knows when participation by some or all members of the committee is appropriate.

TYPICAL GRANT COMMITTEE DUTIES

The grant program committee is responsible for development and oversight of the foundation's grantmaking:

- Develop a grant plan and oversee its execution.
- Give direction to the CEO regarding development of new grantmaking.
- Continually immerse itself in and improve its knowledge of the foundation's fields of interest.
- Regularly review grantmaking strategy and theories of change and recommend changes when indicated.
- Review and deal with grant proposals.
- Make grantee site visits.
- Review grantee reports.
- Oversee the evaluation of the foundation's grant programs, including whether they advance the foundation's program strategy.
- Keep minutes of its meetings and circulate these to the board.

Investment Committee

The composition and role of the investment committee is discussed in Chapter 8 on pages 202–203 and there is no need for me to repeat it here. Instead, I illustrate the workings of a typical investment committee by describing JSF's process.

The investment committee at JSF has regular quarterly meetings plus whatever comes up between meetings. The agenda is developed jointly by the committee chair and JSF's investment adviser, who also attends the meetings. Three of the four regular meetings are virtual and take about two hours each. An in-person meeting is held once a year, and this is usually combined with one or two presentations by investment managers. This one lasts half a day. Materials are circulated a week before the meeting.

In most years business can be managed in the quarterly meetings but during periods of turmoil (2020, 2008–9) or when the committee is conducting a special task, such as a review of its performance or that of its adviser, more meetings are necessary. The committee's authority comes from the foundation board and is subject to the board's investment policy, which prescribes asset allocation. For example, the target for fixed income is 12 percent and the range is from 10 to 20 percent. If bond holdings dip below or exceed the allowable range, the committee must either remedy the situation or ask the board to revise its policy. The committee's minutes detail and describe the state of the foundation's investments, the committee's deliberations and actions, and the advice of its consultant. They are circulated to the board in the monthly report following each meeting. At board meetings, the committee provides a thorough report to the board, together with any request for an amendment of investment policy.

The foundation investment committee has a fiduciary duty to invest prudently. If the committee understands institutional investing, retains a reputable adviser, considers advice carefully, and acts reasonably, then it should not have difficulty satisfying its fiduciary duty. A problem may arise if the investment committee charts an independent path that leads to poor investment returns. Prudent investor requirements vary, and the investment committee should understand the statute in its state or province, get legal advice on the boundaries of prudent investing, and act accordingly.

TYPICAL INVESTMENT COMMITTEE DUTIES

The investment committee is responsible for development and oversight of the foundation's investment strategy:

- Develop an investment policy and recommend it to the board; review periodically and recommend changes when advisable.

- Oversee the investment of the foundation's investments with the advice of an investment adviser.

- Meet at least quarterly to review the foundation's investment performance and its compliance with investment policy and make whatever changes are advisable.

- At least every five years, review the foundation's investment performance and that of its adviser and take whatever further action seems advisable.

- Continually monitor the foundation's investment returns and report them to the board monthly.

- Keep minutes of its meetings and circulate these to the board.

Governance and Nominating Committee

The governance and nominating committee is a foundation's most important committee. It recruits and evaluates the board, among other things. The importance of recruiting has already been noted, and I will add only this. For foundations that plan to span generations, a foundation must build a board that will perpetuate its values and mission long after its current directors are gone. This is a foundation's single most important and difficult task. The entire foundation board should be involved in recruiting but under the committee's leadership.

Most people consider it an honor to sit on the board of an endowed foundation and participate in its good work. So where do you look? Former grantees are good places to look for prospective board members. They are familiar with the foundation and their interests are aligned with its mission. The foundation has had an opportunity to work with them and to get an idea of who they are and how they would fit.

JSF's recruiting from its grantmaking fields of interests has yielded very positive results. Sherry Salway Black, an enrolled member of the Oglala Sioux tribe from the Pine Ridge Reservation, is a board member and JSF's vice president. I first met Sherry in the early 1990s when she was vice president of First Nations Development Institute. She was an invaluable source of information about reservations, tribal colleges, and American Indian economic development.

In 2006 I asked Sherry to serve on JSF's board. I wasn't sure if she would have the time or the interest. If fact, Sherry was honored to serve and wholeheartedly threw herself into it. Her credentials in Native American economic development and broad experience with tribal businesses and nonprofits throughout the country were a perfect fit with JSF's mission and strategy.

King Jordan was the first deaf president of Gallaudet University, a JSF grantee, and when King retired from Gallaudet, we recruited him to our board. King is a much-loved and -admired role model for deaf people all over the world. At a JSF meeting years ago, an interpreter tripped on the carpet and broke two ribs. She resisted going to the hospital because she did not want to miss out on the opportunity to interpret for King Jordan!

King and I made many site visits together, and he was always the one that people wanted to meet. On one visit, a university professor gave me his camera and asked that I take his picture, shaking hands with King. Later, when the professor and I were alone, I asked him why he was so starstruck. He explained, with some emotion, that King had inspired him to get his PhD. Before King became president of Gallaudet, the professor doubted whether a deaf person should aspire to a career in academia.

Bea Awoniyi was the head of disability student services at Florida State University and president of the Association on Higher Education and Disability (AHEAD). Florida State University was a JSF grantee, and we worked with Bea for many years. We knew that she was extraordinary and, when she left Florida State, we recruited her to serve on the board. Bill Corwin was the president of Clarke Schools for Hearing and Speech, a foundation grantee, for nine years. Clarke had a venerable 150-year history but badly needed to reform its vision, operations, and financial affairs. We saw Bill do this with determination and grace. When he left Clarke nine years later, we were on his doorstep.

When Hugh Brown, JSF's longtime investment expert, approached the end of his time on the board, he helped JSF recruit Mike Miller, a financial analyst with extensive philanthropic experience, to the board. Mike had recently retired as director of equity research at the

Bank of Montreal and had also served for ten years as BMO's global head of equities. He now teaches finance at McMaster University's DeGroote MBA School and is a perfect fit on JSF's investment and grant committees. In 2023, JSF recruited Angelique Albert, CEO of Native Forward Scholars Fund, to the foundation board (Angelique, and her connection with JSF, are discussed further in Chapter 9).

Sherry, King, Bea, Bill, Mike, and Angelique have brought their contacts, relationships, knowledge, ideas, talent, and reputations to JSF's board. I am still amazed by how much better they have made JSF.

Recruiting people that you do not know well is rarely a winning strategy. For that reason, I would advise against using professional search firms. You may also get credible candidates on the recommendation of other board members or trusted friends of the foundation. Again, it is important that the candidate is well known by the person recommending. Regardless of how you find them, candidates must be thoroughly vetted and introduced to the board before being invited to serve.

Your foundation should recruit board members according to its needs. The committee should keep a description of the skills and experience of current board members and ask itself, "What expertise does the foundation need in this new board member?" The committee should have written criteria for prospective board members that have been reviewed and approved by the board. This will focus it on the people that the foundation needs and help it to resist unqualified candidates, who may have been suggested by family or other board members.

At JSF, prospective board members are recommended on a form, completed by the person making the recommendation. The form is received and considered by the committee, which decides whether it is interested. If so, it will obtain the résumé of the potential candidate. If, after reviewing the résumé, the committee wants to proceed, the next step is a discussion with the candidate. After that is an invitation to a meeting, usually the grant program committee and dinner afterward. The final step is a board discussion and a motion to extend an invitation to join the board.

Evaluation of board members is also a vital committee function. There should be a process to interview, discuss, evaluate, and re-elect board members every two or three years. Board members who do not make a significant positive contribution should not be re-elected. This is painful, but the board's continued good health depends upon it.

The governance committee should lead regular evaluations of the board. This can be done in summary form after every board meeting by a brief survey of board members and key staff and more formally every three years, often in concert with the CEO evaluation. In those cases, input and guidance from a consultant is invaluable.

The governance committee oversees orientation of new members and continuing education for the board. Another responsibility is keeping the foundation's bylaws and policies current and in step with evolving foundation practice. This is a thankless job but necessary. Otherwise, the foundation will find itself out of compliance with its bylaws and policies.

Except for community foundations, I do not advocate term limits. Getting the right person on the board is difficult and time consuming, and it takes many years to ascend the grantmaking learning curve. The kind of board members you want on your foundation have a great many other choices. If you are lucky enough to have them on your foundation's board, it makes no sense to lose them because of term limits. I do recommend age limits, however, to keep the board vibrant. At JSF the mandatory retirement age is seventy-five.

TYPICAL GOVERNANCE AND NOMINATING COMMITTEE DUTIES

The purpose of the governance and nominating committee is to assist the board to recruit and retain effective board members and to assist good foundation governance:

- Identify board needs in terms of program and investment skills, board experience, and commitment.
- Identify potential board members.
- Recruit, screen, and nominate potential new board members to the board.
- Review the performance of existing board members and decide whether to recommend reappointment.
- Oversee the orientation and ongoing professional development of board members.
- Oversee a board evaluation process on a regular basis to support the board in its effort to be as effective as possible.
- On an as-needed basis (every three to five years) conduct a review and re-evaluation of bylaws, and of committees and their charges, in consultation with the CEO.
- Keep minutes of its meetings and circulate these to the board.

BOARD MEMBER CRITERIA

Note: These general criteria should be used along with the "Board Profile for Recruitment" and any current priorities the foundation is seeking in recruiting new board members. The governance and nominating committee should have a conversation with the full board regarding any current priorities before beginning any recruitment.

- A strong interest in the foundation's mission. A demonstrated interest in one or more of the foundation's areas of programming would be desirable but is not required.
- Should have previous board or volunteer experience.
- A history of successful business or nonprofit experience would be helpful.
- Should demonstrate a collegial and collaborative approach to decision making.
- Willingness and ability to devote at least one hundred hours per year to foundation business.
- Willingness to take advantage of continuing education opportunities.
- Should not be directly associated with any current foundation grantee.
- Should not be an immediate family member of a current board or staff member.

Compensation Committee

This is a touchy subject in any organization, but particularly so in foundations. The philanthropic sector has had its share of scoundrels and there are notorious cases of excessive compensation. These tarnish philanthropy and threaten its independence. A good compensation committee and process will safeguard your foundation and its reputation. The compensation committee must be independent of paid staff and should consider enlisting members from outside the board.

A private foundation is permitted to pay reasonable compensation to its directors, staff, and consultants for necessary services. The board determines compensation policy, and the compensation committee opines on what compensation is reasonable and recommends it to the board. Committee deliberations should be documented and supported by evidence, usually industry compensation surveys and professional advice. Board policy must balance the need to attract and retain good talent with the fact that foundations exist to serve the public interest.

Some people hold that service to a philanthropic foundation is a privilege, and compensation should be either low or nonexistent. They would pay staff at the low end of the spectrum and little or nothing to board and committee members. The contrary view is that you get what you pay for. An effective foundation expects excellent performance from its CEO and senior staff and should reward them with compensation above the median. Similarly, if you expect high performance from your board, then it seems reasonable to compensate them, particularly if your recruiting is not confined to wealthy people.

About 25 percent of private foundations compensate their boards. The size of a foundation seems to be a determining factor and larger foundations are more likely to compensate.

The real question is not whether a foundation pays directors but what value the foundation is getting. A foundation gets poor value from low-paid staff who perform at a low level or unpaid directors who do not do much. One foundation that I admire pays its board members well above the median, at the insistence of its founder. What the founder wanted in exchange was that the foundation would be the board member's biggest commitment, after family and career. An allowance for director's discretionary grants can be useful for foundations who wish to reward directors for service but cannot bring themselves to pay them. Ultimately, your foundation's policy on compensation will reflect its unique circumstances, culture, and values.

I need hardly say that the ability to compensate board members is another incident of privilege enjoyed by private foundations. Compensation for community foundation directors is prohibited. In fact, money usually runs in the opposite direction. Board members frequently donate their money, in addition to their time and talent. Nonprofit boards are similar. Yet the same arguments can be advanced for compensation in those organizations. As I have said elsewhere, foundation leaders need not apologize for their privilege, but they should be mindful of it.

In Canada, the laws surrounding board compensation apply to both foundations and nonprofits. Directors cannot be compensated for holding office but can be paid a reasonable amount for rendering a necessary service. For example, if a director also functions as a foundation's accountant (not recommended) then the foundation could pay a reasonable amount for the accounting service. Or a director could hold a job within the foundation, such as executive director, and be reasonably compensated. Some Canadian provinces, however, prohibit compensation of directors.

TYPICAL COMPENSATION COMMITTEE DUTIES

The purpose of the compensation committee is to assist the board in the discharge of its oversight responsibilities for compensation:

- Annually formulate recommendations and grant compensation adjustments, if any, for the CEO, the board chair, and other directors. In formulating its recommendations, the committee should review inflation and foundation industry salary data and may retain and seek advice from professional consultants. The board has authorized the committee to grant annual CEO salary increases/decreases based on the cost of living, without further board approval.

- Annually report recommendations to the board regarding compensation adjustments, if any.

- Keep minutes of its meetings and circulate these to the board.

Audit and Risk Committee

The audit and risk committee oversees the foundation's financial affairs to ensure prudent management and regulatory compliance. As the name suggests, it also reviews risk issues such as insurance, cyber security, and weakness in financial procedures. The committee should be chaired by someone with financial management experience and can be bolstered by outside members such as professional accountants or legal counsel.

At JSF the audit committee meets quarterly. It reviews and questions the foundation's financial transactions, including bank and credit card statements, to ensure that they are in order. It retains the auditors and meets with them at least annually. Part of that meeting is out of the presence of staff, which allows the auditors to speak freely if they have reservations about staff competence or conduct. JSF's auditors verify investments and report on risk issues, and this information is passed along to the investment committee. The audit and risk committee does not oversee JSF's investment performance.

The CEO is not a member of this committee but attends, with the financial officer, to provide information and answer questions.

TYPICAL AUDIT AND RISK COMMITTEE DUTIES

The audit and risk committee is responsible for oversight of the foundation's financial affairs to ensure prudent management, compliance with legal and regulatory requirements, and a regular review of risk issues (e.g., cyber, insurance). Supervision and review of investments and investment managers is a responsibility of the investment committee, not the audit committee.

- Meet quarterly and review financial reports and activities on a regular basis.
- Review and recommend to the board of directors the hiring of outside auditors and tax preparation consultants.
- Meet with the auditors to review the annual audit report and any recommendations from the auditors.
- Review the annual federal and state (or provincial) tax returns.
- Ensure adequate insurance coverage for foundation and board.
- Ensure cyber security.
- Ensure staff internal control activities are adequate and being followed.
- Keep minutes of its meetings and circulate these to the board.

Executive and Finance Committee

This committee usually comprises the board chair, vice chair, treasurer, secretary, and CEO. At JSF its primary role is to handle foundation business that arises between board meetings. When things are running properly, the CEO attends to this business, and meetings of the committee are unnecessary. When something arises that the CEO, in consultation with the board chair, needs help with, a meeting is called. The second role of the committee is to review the draft of the foundation's annual budget.

A foundation needs an executive committee to act for the board between meetings, should that be necessary. However, it must be careful not to create a board within a board, where foundation business is discussed and resolved in the absence of the full board. For that reason, JSF has expressly limited the powers of the executive and finance committee.

Many foundations have separate executive and finance committees. JSF combined them because their workloads were very light.

TYPICAL EXECUTIVE AND FINANCE COMMITTEE DUTIES

The purpose of the executive and finance committee is to serve as the agent of the board to address foundation business between regular board meetings. The committee also provides oversight of the foundation's financial strategy, reviews financial reports, reviews the draft annual budget prior to its presentation to the board, and keeps minutes of its meetings and circulates them to the board.

The Committee shall have the authority to act for the board and to perform board duties and exercise board powers on all matters except for the following, which are specifically reserved for the board:

- Unbudgeted grants or expenditures exceeding $50,000.

- Amendments to the foundation articles of incorporation or bylaws.

- Amendments to investment policy or major departures from established foundation investment strategy.

- Changes in the foundation purpose or mission or major departures from established foundation grant priorities.

- Hiring and firing of the CEO.

- Board member selection or termination.

- Approving a plan of merger or dissolution, or disposition of all, or essentially all, of the foundation's property.

KEEPING YOUR FOUNDATION HEALTHY

The following are governance practices that JSF has used to keep itself fit. It is not, and cannot be, an exhaustive list. I commend any practice that focuses attention on the foundation's work, the process for doing that work, and the ability of board and staff to attend to it.

Ensure Transparency with a Monthly Report to the Board

I have made the point that foundations should be transparent to the world around them, especially grantees and potential grantees. Transparency starts at home. Staff and committees should report their activities to the board promptly, financial and grant program information should be continually disclosed, and CEOs, or board leaders in foundations without staff, ought to keep the board apprised of their work. Transparency improves performance and pride in a foundation's work.

An excellent tool for internal transparency is a monthly report. At JSF, the monthly report serves as the main tool for communication to the board between meetings. It gives board members current information on all aspects of the foundation's financial health and operations and tells them what staff and grantees are doing. The monthly report organizes and documents transparency and eliminates the need for impromptu emails and phone calls. It goes out at the same time every month in a standard format, which makes it convenient to produce and easy to read.

The format and monthly schedule impose an external discipline for foundation leaders to prepare and circulate minutes in a timely fashion. Before leaving this subject, I note that accurate, timely minutes of board and committee meetings are a hallmark of excellent foundations.

At JSF, responsibility for drafting minutes depends upon who can do the best job. For example, investment minutes are prepared by a consultant (not the investment adviser) and grant committee minutes are prepared by a staff member who writes well. Other draft committee minutes are written by the CEO or other staff member, except compensation, where draft minutes are written by a committee member. All draft board and committee minutes are reviewed and edited by the board chair or committee chair before they are circulated in the monthly report. After that, they are placed on the agenda for discussion and approval at the next board or committee meeting.

A good monthly report ensures that the directors know what is going on and the CEO can rest easy in the knowledge that they are kept informed.

MONTHLY REPORT FORMAT

Page 1	Message from CEO
Page 2	Financial and investment snapshot
Page 3	Rolling twelve-month calendar

Following pages:

Program information

Operational notes

Announcements

Appendices	Minutes of any board or committee meetings held during the previous month, reports from grantees, notable correspondence, etc.

Retain a Governance Consultant

A governance consultant is like a board physician, and it is worth the work to find and retain a good one. JSF started using a consultant in the late 1990s and has used her exclusively since then. She facilitated our first retreat and every retreat since and all our board and CEO evaluations. She brings wisdom, experience, and other virtues such as neutrality and objectivity. Before meetings she surveys the board and staff and organizes and distills their feedback. This saves time by identifying common ground and can provide anonymity, where appropriate.

The foundation's board consultant is also helpful when a board chair or CEO needs to consult occasionally on an issue that has arisen. Such issues are often troublesome and urgent. A consultant who knows your foundation well can give an informed and professional perspective.

Perform Regular Self-Evaluations

To stay in peak condition an organization needs to regularly evaluate itself and its leadership. This includes evaluation of board members, staff leadership, the board, and the foundation. These evaluations are best accomplished with the aid of an independent consultant.

Identify and Properly Address Conflicts of Interest

Every foundation should have a rigorous conflict of interest policy and strictly adhere to it. Every board member should know how to identify a conflict of interest and what to do about it.

A conflict of interest is not inherently bad or even undesirable. If a foundation recruits from its fields of grantmaking, then there are bound to be directors who are connected to grantees or potential grantees. This goes with the territory. The real issue is ethically managing conflicts of interest.

A board member with a conflict of interest should immediately disclose it and be recused from debate and decisions regarding the matter. It is good practice for a foundation to avoid grantees who employ a board member.

Tackle Pet Ideas Head-On

Most foundations will, at some point, be confronted with a "pet" idea from a board member that is outside strategy. This can be difficult, especially when the idea is otherwise meritorious and comes from a valued board member. However, grantmakers must resist grantmaking that takes them off strategy. Pet ideas from board members are among the most dangerous. The antidote is to adopt a policy in advance that pet ideas are not welcome, and all grant requests must go through the foundation's bottom-up process. A policy banning pet ideas can be accompanied by a small allowance in your foundation's grant budget for matching director's grants or allowing directors to direct discretionary grants. Your foundation should require such discretionary or matching grants to be on mission and the quid pro quo is that a director never champions an idea outside foundation strategy.

Take Advantage of Supporting Organizations

Member-based organizations bring philanthropists together and provide networking, expertise, and occasionally inspiration. There are dozens of national and regional groups and associations in the United States and Canada. In most cases, membership fees are not onerous, and they can be excellent places to learn and meet like-minded people. The trick is to choose the right organizations and ration your time. Otherwise, you can become a professional volunteer and attender of meetings and conferences, to the detriment of your real work.

The following is a list of the organizations with which I am most familiar.

The Council on Foundations

The Council on Foundations (COF) was founded in 1949 and is the oldest of the membership organizations. It has members from fifty US states and from around the globe. Its membership includes foundations of every size and type, including community, public, private, and corporate foundations. For foundations endowed with less than $1 million, dues are $1,000 per year. For those with over $1 million but less than $5 million, $2,500; over $5 million and less than $30 million, $4,000; and so on. For JSF annual dues would be $15,000. Dues top out at $45,000 per year for foundations with $10 billion or more.

COF hosts an annual conference and provides numerous opportunities for members to meet. It advocates for the philanthropic sector and focuses on tighter connections between philanthropy and the federal government. COF provides numerous member services including networking through its Philanthropy Exchange, professional development webinars, legal advice, sector updates, an annual *Grantmaker Salary and Benefits Report and Study of Investment of Endowments for Private and Community Foundations.* COF also offers virtual peer-to-peer communities to help members learn from each other and build long-term partnerships.

COF's membership is 900 foundations, which is half of what it was twenty years ago. Many of COF's members are large and giant foundations. JSF belonged for several years in the early 2000s and it was worthwhile, especially for its new and inexperienced president. Membership dues were higher in those days, and JSF concluded that it would rather spend the money on grantmaking and discontinued its membership.

Exponent Philanthropy

Exponent Philanthropy (formerly the Association of Small Foundations) is a national organization that is newer than COF, less expensive, and focused on supporting *lean funders,* foundations that practice philanthropy with few or no staff. Exponent Philanthropy has grown to over 1,500 members and is the largest membership association in philanthropy. JSF has been a member for over twenty years. Dues are a flat $815 annually or $1,900 for a premier membership that includes legal advice. Either way it is a bargain, especially with the membership perks. JSF buys its director's liability insurance through Exponent at a substantial discount compared to the open market.

Exponent's research, publications, resources, and podcasts are of high quality. It has an excellent foundation guidebook and trustee handbook to help teach those who are new to philanthropy and produces an annual *Foundation Operation and Management Report* that offers key benchmarks, along with data on the evolution of lean foundations. Exponent Philanthropy hosts an annual conference and other virtual and in-person opportunities for foundation staff and/or board members to meet and learn.

BoardSource

BoardSource is a nonprofit support organization with a mission to "inspire and support nonprofit boards and executives to lead justly and with purpose."[112] With more than three decades of experience, BoardSource is the recognized leader in nonprofit board leadership research and support. In addition to its membership program, Board-Source provides leaders with an extensive range of tools, resources, and research data to increase board effectiveness and strengthen organizational impact and serves as the national voice for inspired and effective board leadership.

BoardSource offers unique nonprofit membership programs for all players in the nonprofit sector, including foundations. The Foundation Board Assessment Program (annual membership for foundation boards) has a scaling fee structure ranging from $1,000 to $7,500, based on your annual grantmaking range. BoardSource offers many helpful resources, most of which can be used in conjunction with your foundation's governance consultant.

National Center for Family Philanthropy (NCFP)

As the name suggests, the National Center for Family Philanthropy (NCFP) is focused on family philanthropy and foundations, which are eligible to join as members. All others—consultants, service organizations, financial institutions, and community foundations—may join as partners. NCFP has over 350 family members (there is a list on its website) and has developed excellent educational resources that are aimed at families and family philanthropy. Its educational programs and resources are rooted in a family giving lifecycle, which is a conceptualization of the successive stages of family foundation philanthropy. This is a thoughtful and analytical tool that gives an overview and framework for family philanthropy at a glance.

NCFP offers written materials and webinars with expert speakers on various aspects of family philanthropy, peer networking and learning cohorts, a trustee education program, and a fellows program. It hosts a National Forum on Family Philanthropy once a year, with a comprehensive and relevant agenda.

Membership is by contribution, based upon a NCFP recommendation. For a network member, the recommended contribution is between $1,000 and $10,000, depending on asset size. Foundations can, and frequently do, contribute more and are known as Leadership Circle Members.

Grantmakers for Effective Organizations (GEO)

Grantmakers for Effective Organizations (GEO) is a membership organization to assist grantmakers to be more effective. With this guiding principle, it produces various educational resources including books, articles, tool kits, data, and podcasts. GEO also provides numerous opportunities for peer learning and interaction, which include a biennial national conference of about 800 grantmakers and a half dozen or more smaller learning conferences every year. Its peer networks include place-based and remote learning, a fellowship program, a race equity culture fellowship, a strategic learners' network, and a network of "capacity-building champions." GEO also offers *The Smarter Grantmaking Playbook*, which focuses on grantmaking practices that are most supportive of nonprofit success. GEO has a community of over 500 members.

Florida Philanthropic Network (and Other Regional Philanthropic Associations)

There are regional philanthropy serving organizations in every part of the US. JSF belongs to Florida Philanthropic Network (FPN). FPN's mission is to build philanthropy for a better Florida by convening, partnering, and advocating with foundations and key stakeholders as the voice for the philanthropic sector in Florida.

FPN holds an annual Summit on Philanthropy that offers opportunities for foundations to connect and learn about best practices in the field from experts from around the country and, often, globally. One of the advantages of regional organizations is that they contain organized and active *affinity groups*, which cover specific interests that foundations may want to explore more deeply. JSF, for example, has joined the education affinity group and connected with like-minded grantmakers who are also making investments in education in Florida. Annual dues for regional foundations tend to be less than for COF but more than for Exponent Philanthropy. For example, FPN's dues are on a sliding scale according to assets or grantmaking dollars and range from $600 to $8,000 annually.

Philanthropic Foundations Canada (PFC)

Philanthropic Foundations Canada (PFC) is the national network of grantmakers in Canada and has 135 members. Some of these are small, with endowments of less than $1 million and other members have endowments of more than $1 billion. Collectively, PFC members hold assets of almost $50 billion. PFC supports its members through advocacy for philanthropy with government and in society, peer networking, and learning programs. It hosts an annual conference and several affinity group and learning meetings throughout the year. It offers learning resources, including publications and videos, on almost every aspect of foundation practice. Dues are on a sliding scale, depending on assets.

Community Foundations of Canada (CFC)

Community Foundations of Canada (CFC) is the national leadership organization for Canada's 205 community foundations. Dues are based upon assets. The community foundation that I serve on has assets of about $8 million and pays annual dues of $2,000. CFC provides sector leadership, resources, events, and connection with peers.

Sector leadership includes engagement with all levels of government on issues important to community foundations. CFC administered, through its local members, federal COVID-19 grants to nonprofit organizations throughout Canada. It also administers, through its local members, a national grant program entitled Kia Communities in Motion, in which grants are made to charitable organizations across Canada.

Resources include the Learning Institute, which provides everything from suggested organizational policies to detailed videos on fundraising. CFC offers data, fact sheets, and webinars to its members. The offerings range from basic to highly sophisticated and everything in between. CFC has draft donor agreements and supports its members with advice when agreements are complex.

Peer networking includes a communal email where members can get feedback from their peers. The executive director of our community foundation says that this is one of her favorite features. Canada's community foundations deal with similar issues and are responsive, open, and eager to help each other by sharing their experience. CFC also hosts events throughout the year, including an excellent annual conference.

Candid

Candid was formed in 2019 by the merger of Foundation Center and GuideStar and "connects nonprofits, foundations, and individuals to the resources they need to do good."[113] It has a wide range and depth of helpful information. GuideStar, which is free, will give foundations information on nonprofits and can be upgraded with a paid subscription to GuideStar Pro (these are discussed further in Chapter 6). Candid has a *Learning* website for foundations and nonprofits, and a *CF Insights* website for community foundations. Other websites include *Issue Lab* and *Philanthropy News Digest*. Candid's array of free research and data is impressive.

The Center for Effective Philanthropy (CEP)

The Center for Effective Philanthropy (CEP) has a mission to provide "data, feedback, programs, and insights to help individual and institutional donors improve their effectiveness."[114] CEP is not a membership organization, and it is funded by program revenues and grants from foundations and individuals.

CEP's resources are refreshing for their vigor and relevance. CEP is an industry leader in objective and evidence-based research and analysis and produces high-quality research reports that can be downloaded from its website.

CEP also offers services to foundations for which it charges a fee, such as the *Grantee Perception Report*, described in Chapter 6, an *Applicant Perception Report* (APR), a *Donor Perception Report* (DPR) for community foundations, and a *Staff Perception Report* (SPR). CEP hosts an excellent biennial conference.

Imagine Canada (Imagine)

Like Candid, Imagine Canada (Imagine) was formed by the merger of two predecessors, the Canadian Centre for Philanthropy and the Coalition of National Voluntary Organizations. Its work and membership include registered charities (including grantmakers) and nonprofits, and it aims to improve the operating environment for these organizations to do good.

Imagine seeks to improve knowledge through surveys and studies to ensure that decision makers have the right data. For foundations, Imagine's research and data on giving and public attitudes about giving and philanthropy are of particular interest. Imagine is also a public policy advocate at the federal level, as are CFC and PFC. However, Imagine's advocacy spans the respective interests of foundations and their grantee partners and specializes in issues that unite these sectors. Tax policy and regulation of charities are two examples.

Imagine earns most of its revenue from programming. It has a charity accreditation program, with instruction on board governance, financial accountability and transparency, staff management, fundraising, and volunteer involvement. This is useful for foundations that want to improve their organizations and also to satisfy due diligence requirements for grants to accredited potential grantees. Imagine is considering the addition of a grantmaking component to its charity accreditation program. Imagine also offers certification to caring companies that donate at least 1 percent of their pretax profit. Imagine also has a subscription service called Grant Connect, which is a searchable database that connects grantseekers with potential funders.

The balance of Imagine's revenue comes from memberships and fundraising. Less than 1 percent of Imagine's revenue is from government. Imagine has about 300 members, many of which are foundations. Dues are on a sliding scale and, for grantmakers, are based upon the dollar amount of annual grantmaking. Imagine hosts an annual leadership roundtable and other opportunities for sectoral leaders to meet.

Hold Regular Continuing Education Sessions for Board Members and Staff

Continuing education is one of the most valuable yet underused resources available to foundations. A few years ago, I read the results of a survey of program officers from large foundations that said that most felt that they had not been adequately trained to do their jobs. If program officers from large foundations feel that way, then it is safe to assume that many, if not most, foundation leaders share this feeling. A continuing education program for staff and board is essential.

One component of continuing education should be in-house presentations, where staff and board members take turns presenting sessions related to grantmaking, investing, and other important topics. This can be done virtually at regular intervals, with in-person presentations when the board meets. The process is good for engagement and collegiality, as well as learning.

Continuing education should also be regularly presented by experts from outside the foundation, usually when the foundation is meeting for other reasons. Governance is usually a good topic (boards and staff rarely get too much of that), as is grantmaking.

A third aspect of continuing education should consist of board and staff attendance at conferences and courses related to foundation work. Sometimes a speaker on some aspect of a foundation's field of interest can be inspiring and useful. For example, I heard a presentation by Professor Paul Longmore, who was speaking at a disabilities employment conference. Most of the discussion about employment of people with disabilities focuses on the employer's duty to accommodate and how this can be managed. Professor Longmore's message was that medical treatment and accommodation were not enough to ensure the inclusion and participation of people with disabilities in society. People with disabilities are a minority and there is long-standing prejudice against them, which can only be addressed by civil rights legislation and education. Longmore was erudite and persuasive, and his presentation enlightened me and helped me to better understand a JSF field of interest.

Hold Regular Board and Staff Retreats

Foundation boards and staff should take a day or two every few years to shed their routine and concentrate on one or two fundamental aspects of their work. Preparation is vital. Participants should be engaged in advance and be well on their way in their reading and thinking about matters on the retreat agenda by the time that they meet.

Taking time for a retreat is a big commitment, especially for board members, and your foundation cannot afford to treat it lightly. Foundation staff and/or a board committee should work closely with an experienced consultant to produce a good event. A successful retreat will clarify issues, inspire, and invigorate your foundation.

BASIC LEGAL REQUIREMENTS

Although this book is not intended to address legal issues, some legal duties are so basic that no discussion of foundation governance seems complete without them. The basic principles are the same in the United States and Canada, although there are significant differences in the laws of each country and legal requirements are subject to change. Your foundation should always obtain professional advice on its basic legal duties.

Fiduciary Duty

Board members owe a fiduciary duty to the foundation, which means that they must put the interests of the foundation above all else in everything they do. If you belong to another board or if you represent a branch of a family tree or a particular group, you must put the interests of the foundation first, ahead of your family or group. Fiduciary duty should not be construed in a narrow, legal sense. The same duty that requires foundation leaders to carefully steward financial assets also requires them to prepare for meetings and attend to other foundation work.

An exceptional board should have no difficulty discharging its fiduciary duty; it should be second nature for board members to put foundation interests first and do their best work. There are a few pitfalls, however, and these are some of the main culprits:

1. *Self-dealing:* In the United States, founders, substantial contributors, family members, board and staff members are classed as disqualified persons and may not transact business with the foundation, however fair or harmless the transaction or dealings may seem. The main exception to this rule is that the foundation may pay a disqualified person for personal services that are reasonable and necessary to execute the foundation's mission. Compensation for personal services is, of course, subject to the process set out earlier under the compensation committee. In Canada, there is no prohibition against self-dealing provided there is full disclosure to the board at the time of the transaction, and the cost of goods or services is fair market value or less. Compensation for directors is more complex than the US rule. Remuneration for holding office as a director is

prohibited, but directors can be paid for necessary services they perform. However, some provinces forbid payment to directors. Foundations that want to compensate directors should obtain legal advice.

2. *Foundation ownership of a business:* In the United States, foundations are prohibited from having more than 20 percent of the voting control, beneficial interest, or share of the profits of a business. In Canada, the safe-harbor threshold is 2 percent. After that, there are disclosure and/or divestment requirements.

3. *Paying travel expenses for partners and children:* Unless partners and children have a real (and necessary) role in the foundation's business, there is a prohibition against the foundation paying for their expenses.

4. *Paying pledges or debts that belong to disqualified persons is prohibited.*

5. *Lobbying:* In the United States, foundations are prohibited from lobbying. For details, refer to the discussion on lobbying in Chapter 7. In Canada, limited lobbying is permitted. If your foundation wants to engage in lobbying, get professional advice on what is permitted.

At the heart of a foundation's existence is its exempt tax status. Most of the above rules are enforced by penalties and taxes that are so high that they amount to prohibitions. The list above is far from complete, and the rules are not always intuitive. As noted above, your foundation should obtain professional advice.

Minimum Required Distribution

Foundations in the United States are required to grant 5 percent of their endowment annually. In Canada, the requirement is 3.5 percent on the first $1 million of the foundation's assets and 5 percent on everything over $1 million. Noncompliance can result in the forfeiture of the foundation's charitable status.

Foundations in the United States and Canada are permitted to include grantmaking expenses as part of their minimum distribution. In principle, this makes perfect sense but in practice there is occasional abuse. In the United States, the Foundation Financial Officers Group (FFOG) regularly calculates and publishes an average ratio of grant expenses to endowment size, which is usually around 1 percent. However, there is no right ratio that fits every situation. Higher grantmaking expenses are not necessarily bad; it depends upon each foundation's mission, strategy, and process.

Prudent Investing of Foundation Assets

Foundation directors have a fiduciary duty to invest a foundation's assets prudently. If your investment committee retains a reputable adviser, meets regularly, thoughtfully considers advice, and acts reasonably, then your foundation should have no trouble demonstrating compliance with this duty. The duty may pose difficulties for foundations that choose a more unconventional investment approach. In either event, prudent investor statutes vary according to state or province. Professional advice will inform, guide, and protect the foundation.

———◆———

Good governance is everything. If your foundation is well governed then it will eventually find its way to excellent foundation practice. Every foundation is different and the advice in this chapter must be adapted to your unique situation. That said, the underlying principles of good governance are universal. For foundations with staff, good governance clarifies the partnership and respective responsibilities of board and staff. For foundations without staff, it ensures that the needs of the foundation are addressed and that board members attending to those needs are supervised and supported by the board. Regardless of size or style, if your foundation takes the time and effort to practice good governance then it will build a solid platform for its two chief operations—grantmaking and investing—and for its future.

5

Developing Values, Mission, Strategy, and Vision

With this chapter we begin the move from grantmaking theory to practice. Values, mission, strategy, and vision may sound theoretical, but they are the bedrock upon which your foundation's grantmaking is based. What does your foundation value? What does it hope to accomplish? How? What is its vision for itself and the impact it hopes to have? For some, the answers to these questions seem self-evident, and they will be tempted to bypass or rush through this process to get to the "real work" of making grants. However, it is more efficient—and much more effective—for your foundation to first define itself and its priorities. This chapter discusses the practical steps for it to do so. Identifying potential grantees and making grants follow in the two subsequent chapters.

WHAT NOT TO DO

The founders of JSF did not articulate values, mission, strategy, or vision. They prescribed much of the early grantmaking and likely thought it unnecessary to say more. After they died, however, the responsibility for new grantmaking fell to the board, and the lack of guidance, particularly a mission statement and strategy, was a problem. Should we follow the existing pattern and look for new opportunities to serve Indigenous Peoples and students with disabilities? Or were we free to explore new areas of grantmaking? The grant committee muddled along by trying to choose grant programs that it thought would find favor with the rest of the board and particularly the president. We developed some excellent grant programs in those years, but engagement of the grant committee was not optimal.

JSF is an example of what not to do. Foundations should define values, mission, strategy, and vision before making grants. Our example is instructive for another reason. The path to effective foundation practice is through steady improvement, not perfection. If your foundation is making grants without values, mission, strategy, and vision, it is never too difficult or late to take corrective action.

HOW TO DEVELOP VALUES, MISSION, STRATEGY, AND VISION

Involve the entire organization. The board develops the foundation's values, mission, strategy, and vision, and the staff, if it has one, helps the board. How much help and the kind of help it provides depends upon the staff's capacity. Regardless, preparation is essential and includes learning and reflecting on the history of your foundation and its founders. This preparation should be led by a board committee tasked for this purpose and/or the CEO (for those foundations that have one). The same is true for all grantmaking tasks. As noted in the previous chapter on governance, the work should be managed by a central person or group.

I recommend that a consultant be retained. If I seem consultant happy in my advice for foundation leaders, it is for a good reason. Most foundations do not have a large administrative capacity or expertise and it is more efficient to outsource when the need arises. You need the specialized expertise, input, and independent facilitation of a good consultant. The consultant's role is confined to process and is not to do your work for you. Even more than investment policy, values, mission, strategy, and vision reflect your foundation's unique character. Avoid consultants who would tell you what your foundation's character should be.

JSF's process for articulating its core values, a mission statement, and a grantmaking strategy seems typical, and I will use it to illustrate.

Advance Preparation before the Meeting

In 2002, JSF was eleven years old but most of the original board had turned over and half of its members had been on the board for less than one year. We realized that we needed a mission and strategy to ground our grantmaking. As president and CEO, I led the effort. My first act was to hire a consultant and her help improved the process immensely. I could have done it by myself, but my lack of experience would have weakened it. Further, because she was not part of the foundation board or staff, the consultant lent an air of impartiality to the process.

I interviewed existing and former board members and grantees, reviewed documents, and considered the life experience of our founders. I tried to distill the events, beliefs, and aspirations that led to the formation of JSF. Our consultant suggested that we articulate the core values of JSF, and the wisdom of this suggestion became increasingly apparent as I learned more. By core values I do not mean universal values such as *integrity* or *humility* or *service*. I mean values that were particular to our founders, foundation, and board, and that would help define JSF's unique character.

The consultant and I prepared a brief history, a draft statement of core values, and a survey. We sent these to the board and staff, together with other relevant foundation documents such as bylaws, committee charges, and current grant profiles. Board members and staff were asked to review the package, reflect on their grantmaking experience with JSF, complete the survey, and return it to the consultant, who then collated the results without individual attribution. This was important because we wanted observations and suggestions to be weighed on their own merits and not according to the status of whoever made them. One month before the meeting, an agenda and supporting documents including the survey results were sent to each board and staff member.

Our meeting took a full day and was led by our consultant. It was preparation that unleashed the board's potential to consider and discuss values, mission, and strategy. We didn't open the meeting with "what should our mission statement be?" We might as well have asked the board, "What is the meaning of life!" Instead, we approached the mission statement with a discussion of the events that had led the foundation to this point and the ideas and values behind them. Every foundation has a history. Embrace it, learn from it, and use it.

Core Values of JSF

The meeting began with JSF trying to capture its unique history in its core values before building on those to develop its mission and strategy. We are guided by these same core values to this day.

Mandate

Our Foundation was created from the fruits of the free enterprise system operating in a free and democratic society. We believe that the free-market system is the best in the world, but we recognize that some people fail to benefit fully from the system through no fault of their own. It is these people that the Foundation seeks to assist. Specifically, our mandate is to serve the disabled, Indigenous peoples, and those people who are disadvantaged because of their social or economic circumstance.

Education

We choose education because we believe that it is the best means to empower people to become more independent and to participate more fully in the benefits of our society.

Strategy

Our responsibility is to execute the Foundation's education programs effectively and to develop new ones. Understanding that our resources are limited, we concentrate our efforts for the greatest effect. We also constantly re-evaluate and improve our programming and change or replace non-core programs when we find alternatives that offer a better combination of value and effectiveness.

Programs

To maximize the impact of our new programs, we feel an obligation to do more than provide scholarship aid to needy individuals. We also seek to identify niche areas which may have been overlooked or underfunded by other educational foundations. We seek ways to amplify the impact of our programs through cooperation with other organizations.

Partnership

We realize that our programs are, at best, a catalyst. The people we seek to assist and the organizations that serve them do the real work of change and are usually the best source of ideas for new program initiatives. We look to them to help us understand how to make our work more effective, and, whenever we can usefully do so, we engage them as partners.

Risk Taking

Just as the free-market system fosters progress through innovation, the Foundation hopes to employ innovative programs to achieve its goals. Cognizant of the fact that innovation always carries with it the risk of failure, we will proceed only after careful evaluation and will monitor our programs closely as they progress.

Stewardship

The Foundation is intended to be a perpetual body, and it is our responsibility to improve it with each succeeding generation. We attempt to do this by creative programming, vigilant oversight of existing programs, and careful nurturing of our organization and its financial assets. The Foundation seeks to grow its assets over the long term by achieving at least an annual rate of return of 5 percent plus the annual inflation rate.

People who knew Mr. and Mrs. Johnson and the foundation would have easily recognized these values. The value of free enterprise was based upon Mr. Johnson's experience with UPS. He understood and benefitted from the free-market system. Mr. and Mrs. Johnson understood that the system isn't perfect, and that luck plays a large part. They realized that when Mr. Johnson applied for a job at UPS that he had been in the right place at the right time. The Johnsons understood that they had been lucky with money and resolved to use their wealth to help people who hadn't been as lucky with money. The values to serve people with disabilities, Indigenous Peoples, and those in financial need came from core programming prescribed by the Johnsons. Mr. and Mrs. Johnson had been philanthropic and open about their views, and this helped us to understand the motives behind these programs.

Education was another obvious value. Mr. and Mrs. Johnson both had university degrees. Education was Mr. Johnson's ticket to a job at UPS and a key to his successful career. Risk taking was another easy value to identify. JSF owed its existence to Mr. and Mrs. Johnson concentrating their retirement nest egg in UPS shares, in the face of conventional advice to diversify.

The values of *strategy*, *programs*, *partnership*, and *risk taking* reflect the board's view of good practice and were consistent with the values that we had inferred from our history of Mr. and Mrs. Johnson. The value of partnership reflects JSF's business model. JSF does not award scholarships to individuals. It makes grants to partner institutions and nonprofits that award scholarships according to previously decided criteria.

The statement that "we feel an obligation to do more than provide scholarship aid to needy individuals" finds its justification in the non-scholarship grantmaking that was originally prescribed by our founders and the board's realization that scholarships are not always the best way to help people to obtain education. The last value, *stewardship*, acknowledges that the Johnsons had intended JSF to be a perpetual foundation and it is therefore the board's obligation to steward the foundation's assets so that, at the least, the foundation retains its asset base, adjusted for inflation.

PERPETUAL OR LIMITED DURATION?

This decision was made for us by our founders, but many foundation leaders will need to face it, as part of their foundation's vision. The weight of current opinion favors limited duration, although most foundations have chosen perpetuity. There are good arguments on both sides.

The case for limited duration is that foundations should meet present need and let the future take care of itself. Further, foundations that continue through multiple generations tend to drift away from their intended missions and lose their passion and vitality. Employees of large, perpetual foundations have been derisively called *philanthrapoids*, going through the motions of philanthropy because there is money to support them.

Proponents of perpetual foundations can say, with equal justification, that there will always be need. In a society that consumes more wealth than it produces and borrows heavily from the future, it is right to steward assets for the benefit of future generations, as well as our own. Further, if foundations begin with a date certain for their termination, they may spend most or all their endowment before they learn to become effective grantmakers. A perpetual foundation is free to focus on the long term in both its grantmaking and its investing. There may be differences in opinion whether this is helpful for grantmaking, but a long-term approach helps to produce better investment returns.

Your choice between perpetual and limited duration should be influenced by the values, mission, strategy, and vision of your foundation. For a scholarship foundation, a perpetual horizon makes sense. We can suppose that there will always be students with financial need. However, foundations with other purposes may come to different conclusions. For example, an environmentally focused foundation may decide that the need to act now outweighs the desire to make grants in the future. Similarly, a foundation with a mission to promote democracy and a civil society might give more weight to the urgency of the present than the future.

Community foundations almost always have perpetual horizons because they envision permanent service to their communities.

Mission and Strategy of JSF

After we had reviewed the history (which included the prescribed grantmaking of our founders) and agreed on the foundation's core values, the mission statement was easy to write. JSF's mission statement is this:

> Our Foundation exists to serve people with financial need by assisting them to obtain education and employment.

We opted for brevity and tried to craft a mission statement that would convey the unifying theme of JSF's grantmaking. *Financial need* is a broad net, and we adopted a strategy, which reflected our past and present practice of serving Indigenous Peoples of the United States and Canada, people with disabilities, and underserved people.

Most of our earlier grantmaking was premised on an unarticulated and simple theory of change. A theory of change is exactly what it sounds like. You postulate the effect that your grants will have. If the foundation does *this*, then the result will be *that*. JSF's theory was that if it made scholarship grants to people in financial need then they would obtain postsecondary education and better jobs. JSF's theory for serving Indigenous Peoples was different. It focused on business education at tribal colleges and postulated that this would contribute to economic development on reservations. With these theories, the board of 2002 established a guide for evenly dividing the foundation's resources among the three groups it sought to help.

The strategy was rudimentary but what a world of difference it made! We now had a guide. Everyone knew what to expect and what was allowed. The grant committee and staff were free and confident to introduce new grant ideas. Mission and strategy gave us a framework to debate the relative merits of competing ideas.

JSF's mission has been constant since 2002 but its strategy has evolved. Presently JSF has an overall strategy and further sub-strategies for each of its three areas of interest. The overall strategy is brief and is premised on the *theory of change* implicit in JSF's mission; namely, that education will help people to get better jobs and participate more fully in society. I paraphrase:

> Individual overcomes barriers and obtains education and successfully completes educational goals then obtains meaningful employment and then participates more fully in community, whereby community is strengthened.

I further illustrate with JSF's sub-strategy for service to people with disabilities, and again I paraphrase:

Grantmaking serving people with disabilities

The purpose of this grantmaking is to help people with disabilities overcome barriers to both education and employment.

If people with disabilities are given assistance to obtain education and employment, then they will obtain meaningful jobs and participate more fully in society.

JSF assists people with disabilities indirectly by making grants to schools, postsecondary institutions, and nonprofit organizations that serve them. These schools, institutions, and organizations are essential partners, and it is JSF's strategy to help them grow and become stronger so that they can better serve people with disabilities.

Assistance will include scholarships, endowments, mentoring, tutoring, peer support, and other programs that better enable students with disabilities to graduate from high school and complete a course of postsecondary education.

Because qualified people with disabilities are unemployed in much greater numbers than people without disabilities,

JSF will invest in programs that directly help them to obtain employment.

Expected outcomes are success in education and meaningful employment for people with disabilities and stronger, larger programs and institutions serving them.

JSF's strategies for its other two areas of funding, Indigenous Peoples and underserved people, set out strategies in a similar format. The Indigenous strategy still targets business education and business support as ways to help provide opportunities for students and to help grow local economies. JSF's underserved strategy is like the other two, except that it concentrates more on education, mentoring, and early intervention.

JSF has three areas of educational funding and a different strategy for each one. Would it be a better foundation if it put all its energy and resources into a single category or even an aspect of a single category? I have a friend and colleague who argues that private foundations should be single-minded. If a foundation decides, for example, that education for impoverished youth is important then its mission and strategy should focus on that exclusively. This would allow the foundation to gain more knowledge and expertise and concentrate its resources, which in turn would help to make it a more effective grantmaker.

My friend's argument is logical but ignores the fact that foundations are as idiosyncratic as the people who found and populate them. There is no single right approach. Reducing JSF's grantmaking to one area of education would ignore its history and values, its unique personality. This is true of all foundations. Choose a mission and strategy that are grounded in your foundation's unique history and values.

BABIES IN THE RIVER

In a village beside a river, the people notice something strange. There are babies floating by in the river. Immediately the villagers jump into the river to save the babies and yell out to alert the rest of the villagers, "There are babies in the river!" Soon all the villagers are in the river rescuing babies. But the babies keep coming. After a while, two of the villagers leave the river and start to walk away. The other villagers ask them why they are leaving and implore them to return, to which they reply, "We are going upstream to find out why these babies are in the river."

The "Babies in the River" fable (see sidebar) describes another dilemma for the grantmaker. All around us we see problems that cry out for redress. Underserved students lack the money to pursue higher education. People with disabilities do not have sufficient opportunities in higher education and the workplace. Educational and economic opportunities on reservations seriously lag behind the rest of the country. Should we try to alleviate these problems as we find them? Or should we, like the two villagers, go upstream and search for the root causes of these problems?

The answer lies within your foundation. Going upstream may seem like a higher calling, but you must ask yourself, does your foundation have enough knowledge, money, and time to understand and remedy causes of difficult problems? Does it have the appetite and staying power? Do you want to divert your foundation's time and money from people in need so that you can pursue an uncertain reward?

A foundation's initial strategy may be elementary and even wrong. Grantmaking strategy is difficult to make, especially the first time around. This is no reason to shy away from the task. Any strategy, however weak or deficient, is better than no strategy. As your foundation gains more experience and knowledge, its strategy (and even its mission) may evolve. JSF's evolution of strategy for underserved students is an example.

At first, JSF thought that lack of money was the reason that underserved students did not attend and succeed at college. Our strategy was to build scholarship programs at colleges and universities for students in financial need. These are good programs, but they don't always help the students we are aiming at, the ones who would not otherwise attend college.

JSF has learned that college success requires a host of other ingredients such as a solid academic foundation, faith, confidence, and vision. Many underserved students lack these, and JSF's strategy has evolved to support programs that engage them at a younger age, mentor them, and otherwise prepare them for postsecondary education and, once there, to complete it. JSF's strategy in its other two areas of interest has also evolved as we have gained experience and knowledge.

Evolution of strategy is an important aspect of how foundations ascend the learning curve and get better with practice. A foundation begins with its best judgment of a strategy to advance its mission and makes its grants accordingly. The results and its experience with grantees and others in the field help it to confirm or modify its strategy. The three vital elements are starting with a strategy, following it, and using results and experience to test and improve it.

The Vision Statement

Most vision statements contain a vision for the organization and for what it aspires to accomplish. For example, a foundation interested in helping vulnerable children might have a vision for itself as an important grantmaker and repository of knowledge about vulnerable children. It might also envision a community where vulnerable children are empowered to succeed socially and educationally and to become independent, caring, and contributing adults.

At its 2002 retreat, JSF did not articulate a vision and it has not done so since. I believe that this is an oversight, likely because we have taken JSF's vision for granted. Helping students to obtain education and employment fills a need, which seems infinite. The implicit assumption is that JSF will continue to fill as much of that need as it can. However, I believe that a vision of what JSF might accomplish in its next thirty years would be exciting and useful. Our next grantmaking retreat is in December 2023 and I hope that we will use it to develop and document such a vision.

Just as values, mission, strategy, and vision are unique for every foundation, so is the process for articulating them. I have told the story, warts and all, of JSF's process and you can adapt it to your foundation. The process should involve board and staff (for those who have staff) and be led by key board or staff members, with the aid of a consultant. Preparation is essential and everyone involved should count on a substantial meeting of at least one day. Remember that you don't have to be perfect. Your foundation will learn with grantmaking practice and experience, and there will be opportunities to come back to these documents and improve them.

Regardless of how you do it, values, mission, strategy, and vision provide the framework for your foundation's grantmaking. They give direction and the ability to weigh and compare potential grantees and grant opportunities.

6

The Grantmaking
Process

The steps outlined in this chapter, like those in the previous chapter, are based upon my experience at JSF. The grantmaking process, more than any other aspect of foundation practice, differs according to circumstance, mission and strategy, and style. Some foundations do not accept unsolicited grant applications. Others accept and approve grant applications online. Many foundations use a screening process to weed out and respond to ill-suited applications. This chapter illustrates a single process. Take this illustration and adapt it to your foundation to fit its unique character. This is a time to unleash your foundation's skills and creativity.

Before we identify and meet potential grantees, there is an issue that all grantmaking foundations must face and understand. It is the elephant in the room and its shadow looms large over every one of your foundation's grantee relationships.

THE POWER IMBALANCE

There is a gross inequality of bargaining power between foundation and grantee, which makes it difficult for grantees to trust foundations and therefore inhibits honest dialogue. This undermines the grant-making process and makes the foundation's work more difficult.

Most foundation leaders are aware of this power imbalance but underestimate its magnitude and importance. They think that they can overcome it by being respectful and considerate. They have no idea what their grantees really think and would be shocked to learn that many of their grantees do not value their opinions or advice and some grantees do not even like them. How could this be?

Think of a nonprofit organization that you admire. Probably its revenues do not depend upon the good work that it does. Likely, the reverse is true. More work simply increases the gap between revenue and expenses, which increases the need for grant money, which brings the nonprofit to the door of a private foundation.

The private foundation has no financial worries. It is literally made of money and its continued existence and the comfort of the people working there are unrelated to competence or reason. Imagine how galling it must be for a dedicated (and likely underpaid) nonprofit executive to have to ask a private foundation for money. Put yourself in that position. Now think again. You still do not grasp the depth of it.

My Epiphany

I finally understood the power imbalance during a five-day course for philanthropy leaders at the Stanford School of Business in 2007. On the third morning, a social psychologist led an exercise that required the class to negotiate and trade poker chips. After the first round of negotiations, she divided us into three groups, which were tiered according to how many chips each of us had accumulated.

A second round of negotiations and trading followed. This time, unbeknown to the participants, it was rigged to ensure that the top group got the most chips and maintained its dominant position. In the third and final round, the top group was allowed to make up the trading rules, leaving the two lower groups at its mercy. At stake were two small and inconsequential prizes, which would be awarded to the individuals with the highest chip totals. I still remember vividly how we in the top group empathized with the plight of the two lower groups. We designed the new trading rules so that they could get more chips (but not so many that they would displace us) and decided that one of the prizes should go to one of them.

After the exercise and the awarding of the two prizes, there was a debriefing and discussion. The lower groups, especially the bottom group, were genuinely angry with the top group. They felt that the changes we made to the trading rules were inadequate and that we should have given them both prizes. The lower groups also expressed hurt for many lesser (and in my opinion, imagined) slights.

Those of us in the top group were astonished. We had been given the right to set whatever rules we wanted for the final round of trading. Instead of using our advantage to exploit the lower groups, we tried to help them. We even gave up one of our prizes. These were our classmates, fellow philanthropists, and friends. Why were they angry? How could they be so unreasonable?

In the afternoon, with no explanation, we were treated to a guest panel of chief executives from three well-known and respected non-profit organizations. They talked candidly about their dealings with foundations, mainly with program officers of large foundations, and emphasized the unreasonableness and incompetence of these people. One of them asked us, "Do people get stupid vaccinations when they go into philanthropy?"

One executive director boasted of her prowess in sizing up grant-makers and telling them exactly what they wanted to hear: "If they want 'theory of change,' I give them that. If they want 'sustainability' or 'shoes for baby,' I can give them those too. Whatever it takes." Another CEO spoke bitterly about being set up at meetings. When we asked him to elaborate, it seemed that he felt set up whenever people disagreed with him or had data that were contrary to his.

The nonprofit leaders were each confident of their personal integrity, the high worth of their work, and the righteousness of their position. They were genuinely surprised to be perceived as cynical, insincere, and manipulative. They did admit to anger and attributed this to the poor treatment they have received from foundations. They cited egregious examples of arrogance, disrespect, and shoddy dealings, but after listening to these stories, it didn't amount to anything more than the slings and arrows endured by most people over the course of a career.

As the discussion deepened, our guest panel talked about how difficult it is to ask for money every day from people who are financially secure and can do what they please. Surely this is the heart of the matter. Nonprofit organizations, regardless of how good they are, need grants to survive. Most of them are forced to deal with grant-making foundations, which are free to be arbitrary, even foolish. This can cause anger and frustration on the part of nonprofits and can lead to complacency and arrogance in foundations.

It didn't take a genius to realize that the morning's session had been a laboratory version of the problem we heard about in the afternoon.

I realized that there was nothing wrong with my friends and class-mates. They had reacted as anyone in their situation would, and their anger should have been predictable. And if the grantees in our panel were angry then so were grantees everywhere, including some JSF grantees.

Building a More Balanced Relationship

There is no way to eliminate the power imbalance between grantor and grantee. Nor should foundations apologize for their freedom to make grants as they please. However, foundation leaders should ask them-selves if their personal outlook or behavior is a contributing factor to the power imbalance. Has the power of your position gone to your head? Do you sometimes think that your position reflects your high personal worth? Do you ever believe people when they tell you that you are smart, wise, good, or generous? Look at the *I'm not the smart-est guy in the world* sidebar. Do you recognize yourself or anyone else in the foundation?

I'M NOT THE SMARTEST GUY IN THE WORLD

In my former life I spent a lot of time in front of judges. Superior court judges in Canada are well paid, respected, and generally admired. Inside the courtroom, they wield ultimate power and are surrounded by people—lawyers, litigants, witnesses—who constantly flatter them. It is tempting for them to believe what they hear and to think that they were put in this position because they are special or better than most. Logic would tell them otherwise. They weren't special before. How could their appointment to the bench transform them?

Such a transformation seems even more unlikely considering that judges come from the ranks of lawyers, who are unpopular, and are appointed by politicians, who are even more unpopular.

Most judges see themselves realistically, but human nature being what it is, some judges come to believe that they are endowed with special intelligence and insight. One of those judges was presiding in court and had obviously misunderstood key testimony from a witness. The lawyer and witness tried to disabuse him, but the judge would not listen. Instead, he bullied them into submission. When you disagree with a judge, the judge gets to decide who is right. At the end of the exchange, the judge gave a self-satisfied chuckle as he insisted on his faulty interpretation and remarked, with huge irony, "I'm not the smartest guy in the world." Everyone smiled and nodded at his joke. Because of his power, no one told him what he needed to hear.

The judge in that case used the power of his office to squelch facts and opinions that did not fit with his faulty understanding. He used power to indulge his desire to appear right, instead of using it to search for the truth.

Good judges welcome opposing views and, when they are persuasive, they accept them. They do not use the power of their office as a personal perk to gratify their vanity. They use it as a tool to assist their search for truth, to do their jobs.

In place of the traditional roles of generous donor and grateful recipient, consider the following:

1. Foundations need grantees just as much as grantees need them. Grantees do the work of advancing the foundation's mission. No grantees, no mission.

2. Grantees are partners in advancing a mission, and they should be chosen with great care. The nature of the partnership may differ with the circumstances. For example, a nonprofit leader said to me, "Our organization has over fifty donors; they can't all be my partners, can they?" Admittedly, this may stretch the concept of partnership, but I think that it still holds up. In many cases JSF is a small donor among many and does not have a meaningful voice in its grantee's operations. But the grantee and JSF are still pursuing a common goal, and each depends on the other to uphold its side of the grant agreement.

3. A foundation should trust its grantee partner and defer to its experience and knowledge. It should ask, rather than tell, its grantee partner what it needs.

4. Multiyear grants provide certainty and enable grantee partners to plan and execute. Where feasible and when a foundation knows its grantee partner well, it should make multiyear grants, which clearly state the amounts, terms, and dates of continued foundation grants and the date and terms of the foundation's exit. It should also establish a reporting and consultation process with regular meetings.

5. Foundations should consider grants that help catalyze change in grantees and make them more independent. For example, JSF has used matching funds to help grantees build endowments to fund programs that advance their missions. This allows us to exit and our grantee partner to continue the work independently.

6. Foundations should make grants objectively, in a businesslike manner, according to mission and strategy. Grant agreements should be reduced to writing and the expectations of both partners made clear.

7. Foundations should deal with their grantee partners fairly. Specifically, they should not alter grant agreements unilaterally or burden grantee partners with unnecessary requests or expenses.

8. Foundations should be open and transparent about their grantmaking criteria and process.

9. For the grantor and grantee relationships to be productive, a foundation and its grantee partner must earn each other's trust.

By practicing these values, a foundation gives up none of its power, except that it commits not to use its power arbitrarily. It promises to deal fairly and openly with grantees. This would be expected from any reputable business partner. These values go both ways and foundations should expect respect, honesty, curiosity, transparency, and business-like behavior from their grantee partners.

All You Need Is Trust

There were several instances, especially in JSF's earlier years, where our grantee partners did not trust us enough to tell us when the work funded by our grant was not working out as planned. I remember a site visit where a three-year grant project had fallen well short of its goals. Discussion was difficult and, at the end of the meeting, one member of the grantee's team joked that they had skillfully avoided our questions. The grant had been made and received in good faith. Honest discussion would have revealed why it failed. Evasiveness and lack of candor, however, signaled lack of trust and the end of this relationship.

I think most of our grantee partners trust us, and here is what it looks like. In 2015 JSF made a grant to Perkins School for the Blind in Boston to build Paths to Technology, an interactive online portal to assist teachers of the visually impaired and their students. After Perkins began its work and learned more, it realized that the initial concept (and the grant agreement) would have to be modified. Perkins advised us of the issue and discussed it thoroughly with us. We agreed and a new agreement was approved. We were not upset. Designing and executing a new program is an iterative process and Perkins' request seemed perfectly natural. We appreciated its forthright approach and thought that it showed a great deal of confidence and trust. As JSF gets better, the Perkins story is more typical. Our grantee partners know that we trust them, and we want our grants to succeed as much as they do.

If you want an honest assessment of how your foundation's grantees feel, the Center for Effective Philanthropy (CEP) offers a service called the *Grantee Perception Report*. For a fee, CEP will survey your grantee partners and produce a report for your foundation. Anonymity is promised to grantees. This is their chance to give honest feedback without fear of reprisal. And it is the foundation's opportunity to find out what its grantee partners really think. The survey is tailored to fit each foundation. A regular *Grantee Perception Report*, say every three to five years, should be part of a foundation's self-evaluation. It will tell your foundation how it is managing the power imbalance.

With that in mind, let's get to the grantmaking process.

IDENTIFYING POTENTIAL GRANTEES

Your foundation's grantmaking strategy will dictate how it identifies potential grantees. For example, a local foundation with a strategy to improve the quality of life in a particular community will identify potential grantees differently than a grantmaker with no geographical limits.

Choosing a grantee is an important task, second only to developing mission and strategy. It may be daunting at first, but it gets easier with experience. Here are some ideas and resources to get you started.

Existing Ideas and Personal Relationships

Foundation leaders frequently know people who are actively involved in their foundation's field of interest. Go and see them. Your place as a foundation leader will give you credibility and open doors. Don't talk about grants. Ask questions. Find out everything you can about who is doing what, what the obstacles are, and what the likely solutions are. This should lead to other people and meetings. Cast a broad net and gradually draw it tighter to suit your strategy.

If foundation leaders already know potential grantees, then put them on a list to be considered. They should be subjected to the same analysis and evaluation process as other grantees, especially if they are friends. This process will lead naturally to the addition of other potential grantees to the list. Compare them. Which ones seem most effective and align best with your foundation's mission and strategy?

You may find that your ideas and opinions change as you get more deeply into this.

Grantmaking Organizations

Regional associations of grantmakers (often referred to as RAGs) are umbrellas for interest-based grantmaking organizations. They exist in most parts of the United States and Canada and can be found through national or regional foundation member organizations. It is almost certain that you will find people who will talk to you about your area of grantmaking and refer you to people and organizations who can help you.

Candid and Internet Searches

Depending upon the size of your foundation and its grantmaking strategy, Candid may be helpful in identifying grantees. GuideStar and GuideStar Pro were discussed in Chapter 4. GuideStar is free and GuideStar Pro requires a monthly subscription.

An Internet search will help you identify nonprofit organizations. The quality and organization of the information from your search will not be as good as Candid's but it may lead you to the website of a great potential grantee. I need hardly emphasize the importance of independent verification.

Consultants

Consultants can and should play a role in grantmaking. In this context, a grantmaking consultant is anyone who knows more than you do.

Nonprofit leaders, government officials, and academics in your field will likely talk and meet with you without charge. Your foundation credentials will give you access, and you will find most people delighted to share their knowledge with someone who wants to help. JSF got advice from Indigenous leaders and educators in the early stages of its grantmaking and later from a national nonprofit organization, First Nations Development Institute. We have also sought and received advice in our other fields of interest, disabilities and disadvantaged groups, from educators, practitioners, and nonprofits. Getting people to talk to us is never a problem.

Hiring a consultant to find potential grantees can also be useful. In 2005 JSF hired a consultant to find potential grantees in the field of disability education and employment. We found her by joining the Disability Funders Network, a volunteer network of grantmakers. JSF's goal was to build a portfolio of niche, higher-risk/reward grantees. The consultant was extremely knowledgeable of people, organizations, and developments in the disability education and employment fields and helped us break into this area and identify potential grantees.

Should you decide to hire a consultant to identify grantees, have a clear understanding of what the consultant will do and will not do. It is natural for the consultant to want to talk to a potential grantee about your foundation and a grant and you may be tempted to allow it. However, foundation leaders should retain ownership of the grantmaking process. How can they be effective if they contract their foundation's grantmaking out to a consultant? Make it clear to your consultant that grant discussions are off-limits.

Convening

Foundations are well positioned to host meetings for organizations and people in their fields of grantmaking. Invitations can be issued to the people and organizations that you know, and advertising will attract others. It is important to emphasize to all participants that this is a meeting to learn about the issues and not to discuss grants. Otherwise, the potential grantees in the meeting may be more concerned about positioning themselves for a grant than participating in objective discussion. A good convening will help your foundation to better understand its field of interest and identify potential grantees.

Website

If your foundation has a website, it should clearly state its grantmaking mission and strategy, the kind of grants it will entertain, and how to apply. An online form can be useful to screen grant inquiries quickly. This spares your foundation and potential grantees the time and effort of presenting and considering ideas that are not aligned with its mission and strategy.

JSF has grantmaking software that puts a short form on its website, which the potential grantee completes and submits. A small group (in our case, staff) quickly ascertains its suitability and notifies the potential grantee of the result of this review (decline or next steps). A spreadsheet is kept that lists and briefly describes the potential grantee, its idea, and a summary of the staff research and decision. The spreadsheet is reviewed by the grant program committee, which can request that the inquiry be further researched and pursued.

APPROACHING AND RESPONDING TO POTENTIAL GRANTEES

If you have decided to approach a potential grantee, then you have formed a preliminary view that this grantee might fit with your foundation's mission and strategy. If it lives up to expectations, an invitation to submit a grant application will likely follow.

Begin your conversation with the potential grantee candidly. Explain your foundation's mission, strategy, intention, and process. Explain that you think that this could lead to a grant, and you need to know more. Unlike the identification process, the prospect of a grant should be disclosed and discussed. This is no time to be coy. Make no promises, however. You must be impeccable, and you must be clear. The prospective grantee is listening hard. You are simply conveying initial interest. The discussion should be plain and businesslike and include, in as much detail as you can provide, your foundation's process. Explain what information you need and what is involved in the grant application. If the application is decided by a committee, tell them when the committee meets and what it will be looking for.

The dollar amount of a potential grant is a difficult issue. On the one hand, the grant should be sized to the need. In most cases this cannot be done at a preliminary stage. On the other hand, it is impossible to talk sensibly unless the potential grantee has some idea of what you have in mind. JSF generally gives a range, knowing that most potential grantees will fasten on the upper end of that range. With a potential grantee we do not know well, we will start small. Bear in mind that most grantees tend to ask for less than they need because they are afraid of appearing greedy and giving offence. Giving a range helps with that problem. It also helps if you tell prospective grantees to ask for what they need, and that you won't be offended if it is more than your foundation wants to consider.

Many nonprofits have development staff, and you may feel that you would rather deal directly with the program people. However, a good development officer will help educate you about your potential grantee and direct you to the right program people.

Choosing Your Negotiating Team

A smaller group is better. One person is ideal and three seems to be the maximum. You do not want to overwhelm potential grantees or confuse them with conflicting views and information. In some foundations, the negotiating group might be led or consist entirely of staff. For foundations without staff, it might be a part of a committee or the board. Either way, this negotiating group ought to have a mandate from the ultimate decision maker, whether that is the board or the grant committee.

At JSF, the CEO leads the negotiating group, and the grant program committee makes the decisions. As CEO, I consulted with the grant committee in the early stages of identifying and evaluating potential grantees. By the time I met with potential grantees I usually had an indication from the committee that it would be receptive to an application from this grantee, should one be forthcoming. I would tell the potential grantee, "The grant committee knows who you are and has given me a mandate to negotiate with you." Or, when I didn't have a mandate, "I don't have instructions from the grant committee, but I think that this is something that might interest it."

Meeting a Grantee and Negotiating a Grant Application

This conversation should take place in person, usually at the grantee's place of business. Before the meeting, you should have visited the potential grantee's website (if it has one) and obtained or requested information about its mission, strategy, history, operations, financial statements, experience, board, and key staff. What JSF requests depends upon the organization. For example, it usually makes no sense to request financial statements from a state university.

Candid's GuideStar is an excellent source of much of the information in the preceding paragraph, and depending upon the amount of grantmaking you do, GuideStar Pro may be worth the cost. You can save time if you start with Candid and then request updated information or answers to questions raised by the Candid data.

Before the meeting, you should know what makes this organization such an attractive candidate: its mission, its body of work, and its people. Be clear about what more you need to know. Who are the board members and staff? Where does it get its money? What other philanthropic support does it receive? Does it receive small donations from individuals? Does it have program revenue? Does it have a surplus of working capital or endowment? The answers to these questions will help form a picture of the organization. None of them will be determinative.

Say, for example, that your foundation is considering a grant and the prospective grantee's financial statements disclose that it has working capital of $15 million. Some foundations would suggest that the prospective grantee use its working capital and walk away. But judgment is premature. Your foundation needs to understand the reason for

$15 million in working capital. Does the potential grantee make a big annual profit? Or does it need the working capital to produce annual income and act as a cushion against hard times? Or if the organization has a big current deficit, you should ask why. It might be an opportunity rather than a negative.

For the meeting you should prepare a draft agenda and whatever discussion materials are necessary and invite input from your potential grantee. In addition to substantive issues, the draft agenda should include your proposed timetable for the meeting. Otherwise, this could be a thorny issue for the prospective grantee. Your host needs to know how long you plan to stay, but it seems indelicate to ask.

I cannot overstate the value of going to your potential grantee's place of business. There is nothing like meeting people at their place of work and, if possible, the people they serve. Face-to-face contact facilitates the serious discussions you need to gauge alignment of interests and the quality of the organization and its people. If you have board members living in the area, it might be a good idea to include a couple of them, if the occasion permits. They should understand that their role is to listen and ask questions, not to negotiate. That is the job of whoever is leading the negotiating team. And regardless of who is there, ask, ask, ask! This is your chance to find out what you need to know, and no aspect of the organization or its business should be off-limits.

If your meeting confirms a promising grant opportunity, then it is time to open that conversation. Discuss the grant application, the size of grant needed, and the use to which it will be put. Would this be a grant for operating support or for a project? What do they need? Reassure your prospective grantee that there is no right or wrong answer to these questions. If you believe that this is a good grant opportunity, then the application should be a cooperative process.

Carefully set out what is required for the application to be approved. If it must be presented to a grant committee, then explain the process in detail including the dates of upcoming meetings and the composition of the grant committee.

In negotiating an application with a new grantee, bear in mind that shorter, smaller grants provide an opportunity to get to know your partner better and further evaluate its capabilities. Larger, longer, and more ambitious grants can follow. You know what the grant committee will want to see in a grant application and have a feel for how it will react. This is a time for open and frank discussion with your prospective grantee. You both want the best possible application, and you should provide whatever help you can. If something in the application presents a problem or if something is missing, say so. Similarly, you should encourage your prospective grantee to discuss problems and ask questions.

PRESENTING THE APPLICATION TO THE GRANT COMMITTEE

What happens at this meeting depends upon your foundation's process. I am illustrating JSF's practice, in which grant applications are decided by the committee. However, in other foundations, particularly larger ones, grants are approved by staff, who report their decisions to the committee.

At JSF, the grant application is on the agenda, and it and supporting materials are included with the committee's meeting package. Committee members have at least a week to review the package and are well acquainted with the grant applications before them. Potential grantees may be invited to attend the meeting to present their applications and ask and answer questions. After the prospective grantee has left the meeting, the grant committee deliberates and decides. The committee should feel free to decline a grant application, and occasionally it will when it sees something that the negotiating team did not. However, if at this stage, the committee rejects too many applications, there is something wrong with the process.

Be clear on when your prospective grantee should expect to hear from you. JSF's grant committee meets on the weekend, and we make it a point to communicate the decision by Monday of the following week. There are three potential outcomes: approved as submitted, approved subject to modifications, and declined. Sometimes the modifications are a change in the grant amount (occasionally the committee approves a larger grant than requested) but more likely they concern the goals.

THE GRANT AGREEMENT

Every approved grant application, regardless of size, is reduced to a written agreement. JSF prepares and sends a draft agreement to the grantee. Typically, it includes duration, grant payment schedule, and respective obligations of JSF and the grantee with dates, goals, milestones, and general terms. The application is usually appended to the agreement. Sometimes a grantee partner prefers its own form of agreement, and if it captures what we have agreed upon, JSF accepts it.

The grant agreement will usually provide for an annual report by the grantee partner on its progress regarding the agreed-upon goals. These should be definite and easily measurable so that both parties understand the report will be short and to the point. This saves the grantee from the arduous task of writing long reports and you from having to read them. Nothing is more wasteful than requiring grant-ees to prepare detailed reports that are not necessary. Where there are key grantee personnel who are vital to the grant, the agreement should require disclosure in the event of their departure.

REPORTS AND EVALUATION

For multiyear grants, the next year's funding will likely depend upon a grantee partner's progress toward goals and milestones specified in the agreement. Often, a grantee partner will not achieve some of its goals. In that case, the real issue is not the missed goals but the reason they were missed. Perhaps the goals were too ambitious. Perhaps they were the wrong goals. It is not uncommon, particularly in new or innova-tive projects, for expectations and outcomes to change. Unintended consequences are not always a bad thing.

Lack of interest or poor performance by a grantee partner is uncom-mon, but it can happen. There may have been a change of leadership; a champion of a project or mission has left the organization. It is also possible that a grantee's priorities have shifted, and your respective interests are no longer aligned. This can happen when your grantee partner has been distracted by a new (usually larger) grant from gov-ernment or another foundation. Whatever the reason, it is your task to understand why, and this requires a close, trusting relationship and honest discussion.

FURTHER CONTACT AND FOLLOW-UP

Follow-up is a matter of art and will differ in every case. Like any rela-tionship you shouldn't seem needy or bothersome, but you don't want to ignore people. Some of our grantees regularly invite us to participate in functions and are delighted when we do. Some want and need moral support, and we contact and visit them regularly. Sometimes a grantee will want a favor or to discuss some issue and possibly get advice. JSF also has grantee partners that it doesn't call or hear from often.

JSF's board meets twice a year, once in Florida and once elsewhere in the United States or Canada. Both meetings are used to visit grantees. These are planned a year in advance and grantees are generally pleased to host the foundation. JSF normally makes a small additional grant to acknowledge the effort that the grantee has made to host it.

GRANTMAKING PRACTICE AND EVOLUTION OF STRATEGY

Grantmaking practice is a constant process of listening, testing, learning, and evolving. Some foundations in their second or third generation ask, "What would the founders want us to do?" In my opinion, this is the wrong question.

Your foundation should be alive and responsive to the world you live in and the people you serve. For better or worse, your founder's input has been captured in the foundation's values and culture. It is the task of the present, not the past, to interpret strategy. As grantmakers gain experience and knowledge, they should constantly examine and revise their strategy. Evolution of grantmaking strategy occurs naturally but is greatly assisted by keeping it on the agenda and adopting internal and external practices to inform and embrace positive change.

Foundations should regularly review their grants and compare them to their strategy. Did your foundation follow its strategy? If not, why? If so, was its theory of change vindicated? If not, why? These questions will nudge you along. The discussions need proper analysis and preparation before meetings, which requires effort on the part of the board, committee members, and staff.

In addition to your ongoing grantmaking activities, regular and structured interaction with experts and other players in the field will aid the evolution of strategy. JSF organizes and hosts annual convenings of experts and nonprofit organizations in its fields of interest. A great deal of preparation goes into these events by JSF and by the other participants. We pay expenses and a small stipend, but the main draw is an opportunity to exchange ideas in an organized forum. The educational benefit to JSF staff and board, and the forward movement of the foundation, is enormous. My successor CEO at JSF has also retained advisers to the foundation for a nominal stipend. These are experts in our fields of interest who meet with him once a year and, in the meantime, refer him to startups and small nonprofits to whom he otherwise might not have been introduced.

The grantmaking process and examples in this chapter are from my experience and show you what grantmaking looks like at JSF. Every foundation is unique and there are different grantmaking methods for almost all of them. I am on the board of the Fundy Community Foundation in New Brunswick, which uses multiple grantmaking processes. Some are driven by staff and others are decided by the grant committee. Regardless of your committee's strategy or style, I recommend that you experiment. Use trial and error to craft processes that suit your foundation and continue to practice and improve them. Immersion in your field will bring you into contact with other foundations and you should ask them about their grantmaking practices.

7

Thirteen More Things about Grantmaking

There is more to the practice of grantmaking than devising processes. The art of philanthropic practice depends upon the people behind these processes and improves with the knowledge of those people. Many aspects of grantmaking are not intuitive and can take years to understand. The following list is not exhaustive but includes my most important lessons.

1. FOUNDATION SIZE

The stories of exceptional grantmaking in Chapter 2 feature a disproportionate number of giant[115] foundations. Ventures like systematic medical research and transforming the continent's public library system can only be undertaken by giant foundations. On the other hand, grantmaking poses challenges for giant and very large[116] foundations that their smaller counterparts do not have to face.

Giant and very large foundations have more distance between their leaders and their grantee partners. The grantmaking process I describe in Chapter 6 is impossible for most of them. A foundation with few or no staff can employ a process where board members and the CEO deal directly with prospective grantees and decide each application. I don't know where the cut-off is, but at some point, as staff and asset size increase, this becomes impossible.

Consider a foundation with assets of $5 million and a grant budget of $250,000 annually. This foundation has either a small staff or no staff and a highly engaged board. How much easier it is for foundation leaders to define their priorities, cultivate relationships with grantees, and make and manage grants. They do not have to manage a large enterprise, only their grantmaking, and they have firsthand information from personal contact.

I used to think that giant foundations could achieve impact just by the sheer size of their grants. But even giant foundations must invest strategically to have impact. Melinda Gates has observed that The Gates Foundation's entire endowment would not be enough to finance the California school system for one year. Gates may be a giant compared with other foundations but not compared to the issues it tackles. Foundations, regardless of size, cannot underwrite social change. They must invest strategically and act as a catalyst. The value of grantmaking depends more upon a grantmaker's strategy and quality than on its size.

2. ADHERING TO STRATEGY

Following strategy will lead a foundation toward new solutions and cause it to take risks and make grants that do not feel safe or familiar.

This is the path to innovation. Note, however, the use of the word *following*. Strategy, by itself, is not enough. Your foundation must follow its strategy for it to have meaning.

Research shows that it is easier for foundations to develop a strategy than to follow one. A survey and analysis conducted by the Center for Effective Philanthropy (CEP) in 2007[117] revealed that most foundations articulate a strategy but do not follow it. CEP randomly selected and studied 21 of the 450 largest foundations in the United States, ranging in size from $100 million to more than $1 billion. The median foundation size was $260 million. The purpose of the study was to find out how foundations use strategy to inform their grantmaking decisions.

CEP defined strategy as a framework for decision making that is

1. focused on the external context in which the foundation works, and

2. includes a hypothesized causal connection between use of foundation resources and goal achievement (theory of change).

The CEO and a program officer from each of the foundations were interviewed at length about the foundation's grantmaking. Not surprisingly, everyone agreed that a grantmaking strategy was important and would increase the foundation's ability to make a difference. And just about everyone professed to have a strategy. All respondents talked about their foundation creating social impact.

But when grantmaking practices were objectively analyzed, there was a discrepancy between foundation rhetoric and foundation action. Only 25 percent of foundations employed a grantmaking framework that would meet the Center's basic definition of a strategy. The remaining 75 percent ranged from having absolutely no strategy to following a strategy some of the time.

The reason most foundations do not follow a strategy is because it is often unfamiliar, uncomfortable, and difficult. It is much easier to follow the path of least resistance. For example, a good friend or a former grantee comes to you with a request that is outside your foundation's strategy. Or a board colleague urges a worthy grant request that is outside the foundation's strategy. It is easier and more pleasing in the short run to say yes to the person standing in front of you, especially when the within-strategy alternative is untried and risky. However, your foundation must be accountable to its strategy if it wants to be effective. This requires discipline, rigor, and fortitude. Foundation leaders must reject comfort. This is the time for objectivity.

Following strategy will prevent a grantmaker from being all things to all people. It will also keep your board and staff engaged and focused on projects and organizations in your foundation's area of interest, which helps build their knowledge and expertise. Following strategy will regularly require a grantmaker to disappoint friends and to say no to potential grantees who do wonderful work but are outside of your foundation's focus. Effective grantmakers say no to grants that do not fit strategy. Following strategy is where foundation leaders earn their keep.

3. THE OVERHEAD MYTH, CAPACITY BUILDING, AND TRUST-BASED PHILANTHROPY

There is an idea that grants for overhead are bad, and grants confined to programs are good. This has fallen out of favor because grantmakers realize that grantees must maintain themselves and that their good health and security are vital. If a grantee partner is performing work that is aligned with a foundation's mission and strategy, then it should not matter whether the grant is for operational expenses or a particular project.

Say, for example, your grantee partner reported that it used your capacity-building grant to help pay for a fundraising campaign. Would you feel that the grant should have been put to a better use? What if the grant helped raise net proceeds several times larger than your grant? Would you be pleased? Your grant has been leveraged and your partner now has more to spend on programs. Similarly, your capacity-building grant could be used to help pay for information technology or a new accounting system. Would you think that your foundation's grant had not made a difference? Think again. Your grant has given a trusted partner the tools that it needs to be more effective.

Recently, I heard a panel of program officers at a meeting of grant-makers. One member of the panel, from a large foundation, admitted that she used to be afraid to make grants for operating support. She was a program officer and if the grants were for operating support, then what would her role be? I thought that she was brave to say this in front of a large group of her peers. The truth (as she knew) is that her role as a program officer would be enhanced. She would still seek out, negotiate, and recommend grants that best advanced her foundation's mission. The difference is she would be negotiating grants that optimize both the partnership with grantee partners and the quality of the foundation's investment.

Grantmakers would all do well to open the conversation by asking their potential grantees, "What do you need? How can we help?" Trust should be a given. If you don't trust, then you should not invest your foundation's precious grant money. Find a grantee partner that you do trust. If that is difficult, then your foundation should re-examine its grantmaking process; perhaps the fault lies there. There is an institute, the *Trust-Based Philanthropy Project*, founded by the Whitman Foundation and other like-minded foundations, dedicated to this subject and its website contains many helpful resources.

4. THE SECRET BEHIND EVALUATING GRANTS

The real secret is that everyone talks about evaluation, but nobody wants to do it. Evaluating grants is a process of weighing quantitative and qualitative evidence, applying reason, and drawing inferences. It is usually difficult and rarely conclusive, especially in the short term. However, if you aspire to effective grantmaking then you need evidence of how your grants are working (or not working), and this means measurement and evaluation.

There is a truism in grantmaking that *not everything that is important can be measured and not everything that can be measured is important*. Sometimes it is easy to know what should be measured. For example, for the Dorr Foundation, measuring the number of accidents on highways with outside lines compared with those without them was obvious and relatively easy. Usually, evaluation is more difficult. Figuring out what to measure and how much time and money to spend on it is an art. A foundation must balance competing interests and make compromises. Money spent on evaluation means less money available for grantmaking.

New grantmakers can be too ambitious and unrealistic in their zeal to evaluate. When I was new, I thought that JSF should obtain the best evidence possible. For example, if we made grants for a scholarship program to help students graduate from a postsecondary institution and get better jobs, then we should find out what jobs "our" students got. I soon learned how impractical and unnecessary this was. It is impractical because of the energy and expense (not to mention the unseemliness) required to track down students and check up on their employment. It is unnecessary because there are national surveys that tell us the employability and the average salary of college graduates.

A less expensive and more practical approach is to know the college graduation rates of our students and compare them with those we do not serve. If the graduation rates of our students are better, then we can infer that they were able to get better jobs. This inference is subjective, but the conclusion seems indisputable. Let us take a further step. If we know that scholarships to students with financial need contribute to higher graduation rates, then do we have to measure the graduation rates of our students? Or can we simply infer that they graduate at higher rates and get better jobs?

At JSF, we have learned to be sparing of evaluations that are difficult to internalize. We do not have much in-house capacity and a written evaluation the size of a PhD dissertation takes time and energy to digest and act on. Over twenty years, we have had fewer than a dozen of these. They require a lot of thought, planning, and expense and are reserved to inform key issues of strategy or to judge the impact of a major investment.

In most cases, a foundation grant is based upon a logical theory but the quantitative evidence is not conclusive. There is likely an abundance of qualitative evidence, compelling testimony from individuals who have been helped or about situations that have been improved.

This brings us to a second truism of evaluation: *no data without stories and no stories without data*. Anecdotal evidence, by itself, is of little value. It must be accompanied by objective (quantitative) evidence. Going back to our scholarship example, if you are providing scholarships to students, how do their graduation rates compare to their peers who do not get scholarships? This number won't prove anything by itself, but together with a logical theory and student stories, it constitutes strong evidence of the efficacy of the scholarships.

Usually, grantees are the ones measuring the results. Part of the grant negotiation should be what measurement is needed and how much, and that should set be out in the application and the grant agreement. In these negotiations, be respectful of your partner's resources and mindful of your own. Progress toward goals will be reported and usually form part of the evaluation. What else needs to be measured? How much text is needed? Pare it down to the minimum.

Sometimes, evaluation is done by the foundation or is the subject of a special grant to measure and evaluate impact. If a foundation has a special knowledge or interest in measurement and evaluation then it will be natural for it to evaluate impact, and this might provide great value to its grantee partner. Most foundations do not have the in-house capacity to conduct evaluations. A third party can be retained, or the foundation can make a grant to build evaluation capacity in its grantee partner. Either way, the grantee partner is the central piece in the evaluation puzzle and evaluation should be a cooperative effort.

Measurement of results and/or evaluation of its program is not the end of the matter. Your foundation must take this information and hold it up against its strategy. Does this grant fit strategy? Does it support your theory of change? If not, why?

5. TAKING PROGRAMS TO SCALE

The definition of scaling is as follows: "social innovations have scaled when their impact grows to match the level of need."[118] This is the holy grail of grantmaking. Grantmakers, especially new ones, have dreams of taking the work funded by their grants to scale so that everyone can benefit. They soon realize how difficult it is.

There are tens of thousands of philanthropic programs doing good in local communities. Some of them are ingenious. The efficacy of many of them has been demonstrated. But they stay small and local. Critics of foundations and nonprofits point to this lack of scale as evidence of inefficiency. They contrast it with the free market's ability to quickly take successful ideas to a large scale. This criticism ignores a fundamental difference between for-profit business and the philanthropic and nonprofit sectors. Most grantmakers and their grantee partners are addressing complex social issues. Just because a program is successful in one area does not mean that it can be replicated like a McDonald's franchise and plopped down somewhere else.

To illustrate what it takes to scale a successful program, consider the experience of a JSF grantee partner, Pathways to Education (Pathways). Pathways aims to help students from economically depressed neighborhoods graduate from high school and transition into postsecondary education or employment. Its mission, informally, is to make Canada a "graduation nation." The strategy is to have parents, volunteers, and Pathways' staff surround students with support and help them to succeed academically. Support includes counselling, mentoring, tutoring, and financial assistance. Student engagement and accountability are key aspects.

Pathways was founded in 2001 and began in Toronto's Regent Park, the oldest and largest public housing development in Canada.[119] It was an area of poverty, gangs, drugs, and frequent gun violence. Young people saw no opportunity and did not stay in school. The dropout rate was 56 percent, and for children of single parents and immigrants, it was more than 70 percent. Government programs to alleviate the problem were ineffectual.

Pathways has achieved dramatic results. Three quarters of Pathways' students graduate from high school and attend college or university. High school graduation rates of the Pathways students of Regent Park are now on par with both the Ontario and the Canadian averages. Pathways has developed a community model and its program is now being delivered to over six thousand students in thirty-one communities across Canada. It is a great success story and has achieved international recognition.

Given its amazing success, why stop at thirty-one communities? Why not put Pathways everywhere and solve the problem of all underserved students not graduating from high school? As enticing as it may seem, this solution is an illusion. It ignores the complexity of both the problem and its remedy.

The founders of Pathways did not flip a switch or stumble upon a magic potion. They took proven social and pedagogical methods and developed a program that would help students succeed. There are similar programs elsewhere that are also effective. One of the largest and best known is Communities in Schools, a US organization.

Pathways was able to succeed in Regent Park because its founders had worked in the community for years and were steeped in it. They understood the social and health problems and how these contributed to academic underachievement. Even then, they did not presume to develop a remedial program. Instead, they engaged the community in a consultation to explore a vision of success and how to achieve it. The community knew and trusted Pathways' founders and joined them to consider solutions to seemingly intractable problems. How do we break the cycle of poverty? What would it take to enable young people to succeed academically and become the professionals and leaders of tomorrow? How would the community support this? From these consultations, a model emerged to provide support in four areas: academic, social, financial, and advocacy.

The founders of Pathways knew that they had a model that could be delivered in other parts of Canada. They devised a system for replicating its service elsewhere and invested millions to that end. The model begins with an extensive community engagement process. Can this program be tailored to suit the community's needs? If so, does the community have the resources to support it? If, after community consultation, it appears that the Pathways model will work, a local nonprofit is licensed, trained, and financed to adapt and deliver to the local community. The program takes several years to develop, and local financial sustainability is difficult (sometimes impossible) to obtain.

The Founders of Pathways, Carolyn Acker and Norman Rowan, were the right people with the right ideas at the right time. In addition to their passion for the project, Acker and Rowan had abilities that helped them to propel Pathways forward. They knew the importance of data and how to collect and organize them. They used data of early success to advocate and attract community champions. They obtained support from the corporate sector and persuaded various levels of government to get behind Pathways.

Let us reconsider the thousands of local programs that we think should be scaled. How many of them have the experience, deep knowledge, and capability of people like Acker and Rowan? Or the resources of Pathways? And, even with those advantages, Pathways will never meet the threshold proposed for successful scaling.

There is another difference that proponents of for-profit-style scaling usually ignore. Commercial enterprises can scale because they offer products or services that people want and are willing to pay for. Nonprofits are usually trying to scale a product or service to be consumed by people who cannot pay for it. This is a much harder sell, even more so because the people paying usually do not even know the people consuming the product or service.

Just because a program is small compared to unmet need does not mean it is unimportant. There is a fable of a young girl on a beach picking up starfish washed up by the surf. She is throwing them back into the ocean so that they will not dry out in the sun and die. A man watches her for a while and then goes up to her and says, "This beach goes on for miles and there are millions of starfish. Throwing a few handfuls back into the ocean doesn't matter." The girl threw a few more starfish into the ocean and replied, "It matters to these ones." Like the girl on the beach, JSF helps relatively few. However, that does not diminish the value of JSF's help to those that receive it.

Grantmakers should not be unrealistic in their expectations from grantee partners. An inexperienced foundation and its grantee partner can talk each other into grandiose plans that have little chance of a successful outcome. In its early years, JSF made a grant to improve nationwide employment rates of people with disabilities. Unemployment among people with disabilities has always been high and has resisted solutions for decades. Our "solution" was funded by a $700,000 grant over three years and failed miserably. It didn't have a chance. It would have been much better to have started small or to have invested in an organization that was already succeeding in a national strategy.

Do not be disappointed if your foundation's great programs are not replicated. Many programs succeed because they are small and local and enjoy the trust and support of their communities. Making them bigger would lose those advantages and cause them to fail.

Taking a program to scale is a noble ambition for a grantmaker. If you or one of your grantee partners has an idea that you think your foundation should scale, do not let your excitement obscure your vision. Be realistic about how it could be accomplished, the likelihood of success, how long it would take, and the difficulties along the way. Do you and your grantee partner have the expertise and capacity to see it through? What further resources or advice do you need?

6. TIME

Grantmaking, like all investing, is not for people in a hurry. It has been said that grantmakers cannot do much in two years but can do almost anything in twenty years. Try to envision your foundation's field of interest after five, ten, and twenty years. What difference will your strategy have made? How confident are you in your theory of change? What evidence do you need along the way to affirm that it is valid and that the programs you are supporting are making a difference? What will you do if that evidence is not forthcoming? The art of grantmaking lies in these questions. You need the faith of fools,[120] but you cannot be foolish.

The area of JSF's grantmaking that best illustrates the value of time is its grants in service of Indigenous Peoples. The strategy was to make grants for business and entrepreneurship education. Our theory of change was that this would contribute to economic development and employment on reservations. We began implementing the strategy in 1995, and in 2003 we formed a task force to study the impact of our grantmaking. The task force was informed by JSF's grantee partners, Indigenous educators and business leaders, and several consultants. Its activities spanned two years and found little evidence that JSF grants had made an impact on economic development and employment opportunities.

JSF affirmed its theory of change, made some changes to its strategy, and kept going. This was an act of faith. JSF believed that appropriate, sustainable development on reservations could only be done by Indigenous people. It also believed in the power of education and in the Native American educators and leaders who were working to effect development and change. Many tribal college business faculties were thriving, and large numbers of students were graduating. We felt certain that there would be trickle-down effect and results would follow. We were heartened by research from the Harvard Project on American Indian Economic Development that reservation economies were growing,[121] and we felt certain that JSF's grants were assisting the people and institutions behind this growth. Almost ten years passed before we had evidence to support our theory of change.

Keeping faith and adhering to strategy are important aspects of grantmaking. Measure and evaluate along the way. Change what isn't working. Reconsider your theory of change and ask yourself if it still makes sense. If so, keep going.

7. PROGRAM-RELATED INVESTMENTS

Foundations are permitted to make program-related investments (PRIs), which are grants in the form of financial investments. Say, for example, a foundation invests in a venture capital fund to support the creation of local newspapers. The real purpose is not to make money but to support local journalism. The foundation would record the investment as a grant and any financial return on this grant would be added to the foundation's grant budget in the year it is received. Depending upon the opportunity, a PRI can be an effective grant. JSF has made only one PRI. It was a passive investor in a fund assembled by another grantmaker. We had no illusions of making money and treated it as a grant. We "lost" 80 percent of the money invested. The 20 percent that was returned was regranted by JSF in the year it was received. If your foundation is making its first PRI, I suggest that it obtain legal advice to ensure that the investment qualifies and is otherwise in order.

8. ADVOCACY

The case for advocacy, in its most basic terms, is that it gives your foundation leverage. Advocacy can help bring about changes in policy, which help everyone. For example, say your foundation believes that scholarships and mentoring for underserved middle-school children will help them succeed and contribute to society. Instead of making grants, which help a limited number of students, it could use its grant budget to fund advocacy for a change in government policy that helps all underserved students. Advocacy becomes a vehicle for a foundation to execute its mission and strategy. It should not be used casually, to advocate for issues outside of a foundation's mission and strategy.

Foundations engaging in advocacy should be mindful of tax rules pertaining to private foundations, which, for practical purposes in the United States, amount to a prohibition on lobbying. The line between lobbying and advocacy is not always easy to recognize. Foundations are lobbying when they attempt to influence legislation at any level of government by contacting lawmakers or urging others to do so. Foundations are prohibited from funding others to engage in lobbying.

Your foundation can safely advocate the virtues of scholarships for underserved children or any other cause, but once specific legislation is under consideration, the foundation must refrain from contacting lawmakers and it must refrain from urging others to contact lawmakers.

Let's say your foundation decides to advocate for scholarships and mentoring for youth from families with low incomes. How should it go about this? Should it embark on an education campaign to show the social and economic benefits? Communication experts tell us that this would be a waste of time and money. In *Stop Raising Awareness Already*,[122] the authors explain the fallacy in the knowledge gap theory of communication.

The knowledge gap theory posits that once people are given accurate information, they will change their beliefs and behavior. But most people hear and believe what they want. They are impervious to cogent information or logic. Instead, they are tribal in their beliefs and will form most of their judgments accordingly. The effective way to communicate with them is to engage them on a subject in which they have an interest. As counterintuitive as this theory may seem, it explains the reality that most people won't be moved by the overwhelming logic supporting your foundation's position on scholarships. They won't even listen.

What you need instead is a focused strategy. Conceptualize advocacy as an ongoing conversation, rather than telling people what to think or do. Your foundation could convene people who share its interest in scholarships. The meeting could include policymakers and legislators. People respond to foundation invitations because they know that foundations, unlike lobbyists, business, or even nonprofits, don't have their hand out. Their actions are guided by a desire to make things better, not self-interest.

Your foundation might also commission research to, first, verify its theory and, second, persuade policymakers and legislators. Put yourself in their position. They want what is best and, in that way, are aligned with your foundation. They need evidence and are more likely to trust it if it comes from a nonpartisan source. This is more so if you have a personal relationship or if the policymaker knows that your foundation has been impeccable in its past dealings.

Advocacy can be particularly effective at a local level by a place-based foundation, which has deep knowledge and experience in the community. The foundation's chair, board member, or executive director may have a reputation and relationships with legislators and policymakers that can be used. Bear in mind that the foundation must speak with one voice and its strategy must be centrally managed. Your foundation's political capital will open doors. Use it strategically and carefully.

Advocacy, like most foundation grant programs, is a long game. Don't expect quick results or dramatic wins. The conversation will usually take years, not months. The story of John Dorr and the Dorr Foundation in Chapter 2 is a textbook example of effective advocacy. The use of research and evidence, engagement of experts and policymakers, and persistence are exemplary. The change in policy—to paint outside lines on highways—was relatively simple and it benefited most Americans. Yet it took over ten years to influence that change. Advocates for scholarships for underserved youth have a much more challenging task.

9. COMMUNICATION

Advocacy and communication are intertwined but, regardless of your foundation's interest in advocacy, it should communicate with the world it is trying to help. A good grantmaker is transparent with grantees and the world. Open the curtains and let the light of day shine! Be open with grantees about your mission, strategy, and grantmaking process. Instruct them on how to apply, how long it takes, what size grant they might expect, and their chances of getting one. Be as straightforward and matter of fact as you can.

Distribute an annual report that tells people about the grants you make and how and why. List your grants and your finances and your investment results. Tell your grantees' stories. Annual reports can be inexpensive and need not be printed. Disseminate the report widely to grantees, potential grantees, policymakers, and other people of influence in your field. Do not expect a wide interest in the report. However, when people hear of your foundation or become interested in it for other reasons, they will read its annual reports to get more information.

Depending upon its size, technical capacity, and grantmaking style, your foundation might maintain a website. In addition to information on its mission and grants, past years' annual reports should be available. The website will not excite interest, but even more than the annual report, it provides easy access and reference for someone who has heard of your foundation and wants to learn more.

Social media—Facebook, blogging, newsletters, and so on—is another way to communicate. Do not think of social media as a megaphone for your foundation to broadcast its good works and opinions but as a place for conversation with grantee partners and their peers about events and ideas in their fields of work. Given the prevalence of social media and its reputation for captivating people, one might expect it to be a game changer. Our experience and industry research show otherwise.

A study by the CEP,[123] showed that foundation social media and communications were generally unnoticed by grantees. It surveyed thirty-four foundations (average size $370 million) and more than six thousand of their grantees and found the following:

- Most foundations (71 percent) use social media tools.

- Very few grantees (16 percent) use social media from their foundation funders. However, most of them (80 percent) used social media in their own work.

- Most grantees who use foundations' social media do it to learn about their foundation partner. However, they find those resources less helpful than traditional communication methods.

What should foundations make of this? First, if a foundation's grantee partners are not using its social media, then probably no one else is. Second, social media won't change anything by itself. If a foundation is not close to its grantees or is not a good communicator, social media will not add value to the relationship. Third, social media may have a place in foundation strategy, but it appears to be a weaker form of communication than direct contact. If you want to communicate with your grantee partners, it is more effective to phone them or go to see them.

JSF uses Facebook, a blog, and an electronic newsletter. Our Grantee Perception Report showed that 32 percent of our grantee partners use our social media, which is higher than our peers but still disappointing. Social media has drawn us closer to some of our grantee partners, and we have continued, albeit with lower expectations. We keep asking ourselves if it is worth it. Like everything else, social media must help us to do our work to justify its expense. For JSF, the jury is still out on social media.

Advocacy and communication should be a natural outgrowth of your foundation's execution of its mission and strategy. They are not stand-alone activities. The best way for your foundation to advocate and communicate is to go about its business of meeting with grantee partners, experts in the foundation's fields of interest, policymakers, and other interested groups and individuals. To illustrate, I will recount an example from JSF that, in retrospect, underlines our (my) naivete at the time about communication and advocacy.

In 2014, JSF wanted other foundations in Palm Beach County to support its local mentoring and scholarship program, which was growing quickly. We convened a meeting, invited local foundations and other interested organizations, described the program and its outcomes, and asked if anyone was interested in participating. The meeting was well attended but nobody was interested in partnering with JSF on the scholarship program. Everyone agreed on the importance of scholarships and postsecondary education, however, and there were some good ideas.

Over the ensuing months, JSF continued to convene the group and a plan for a local college access network (LCAN) was developed. This led to a meeting of the larger community, chaired by JSF, which drew over 120 people and organizations and led to the formation of *Achieve Palm Beach County*, a local college access network. We thought what we were doing—convening meetings and forming *Achieve Palm Beach*

County—was our regular work, not communication. Had anyone asked us at the time, we would have also denied that this was advocacy!

10. PACE OF GRANTMAKING

How long should it take a grantee to get a grant from your foundation? There is a body of best practice literature to the effect that grantmakers should make their grants quickly. The need for money is urgent and grants should not be slowed by red tape. Some tout the virtues of grantmaker agility and use of technology to receive, evaluate, and fund grant requests quickly. In some situations, there is merit to these arguments. During the early months of the COVID-19 pandemic, for example, many foundations, including JSF, made rapid emergency grants to existing grantees based on nothing more than a conversation and an email exchange. JSF was able to make these rapid grants because it was dealing with existing grantees, who had already been through a comprehensive due diligence process.

In this book, I make the case for a slow, deliberate grantmaking process. Choosing a grantee partner is an important commitment. Good relationships and grants can last years, and their effects are often felt for decades or generations beyond that. It takes time and effort to ensure a prospective grantee's organization, people, and ideas are best suited to advance a foundation's mission and strategy. Grantmakers should not apologize for a thorough process. Grants made with insufficient knowledge or thought are likely to be ineffectual.

The pace and process of your foundation's grantmaking will depend upon what its grantmaking is designed to accomplish and the strategy it employs. Local foundations with deep knowledge of their communities and potential grantees may be able to act more quickly. Similarly, some grant strategies are better suited to a summary application process. Whatever your grantmaking pace, do not allow your foundation to become a simple distributor of money. Grantmaker agility is certainly a virtue but impact is the real point.

11. HUMILITY IN GRANTMAKING

Harry Truman's observation—*It is amazing what you can accomplish if you don't care who gets the credit*—has special meaning for grantmakers. A foundation gets more done when it realizes that its business is to advance its mission and not itself. Your grantee partners and the people they serve do the real work to create change and they should take credit for it. When it comes time to take a bow, the foundation should be very much in the background.

JSF recently made a large matching grant to the Tom Shortbull scholarship fund at Oglala Lakota College. The foundation's name will not appear anywhere and students who apply for this scholarship will be unaware of JSF's grant. They are aware of Tom Shortbull, however. He is a founder and longtime president of Oglala Lakota College, a former state legislator, and a longtime champion of the Pine Ridge Reservation and the Lakota People. Who better to inspire those students, Tom Shortbull or JSF?

The exception to this rule is when the reputation of the award adds value. Some notable examples are the Nobel Prize, the Rhodes and Fulbright scholarships, the MacArthur ("Genius Grant") Fellowship, and the James Beard Foundation awards for culinary professionals. There are thousands of lesser-known examples, especially in community-based foundations.

If you are concerned that your foundation's low public profile will hinder its work, don't be. Your grantee partners know and appreciate what you do. If your foundation is immersed in its field of interest, then prospective grantees will have no trouble finding it.

12. PARTNERING WITH OTHER GRANTMAKERS

I have heard countless presentations that extol the advantages of working in concert with other funders. In response, I would extol the virtues of originality and independence. That said, it must be acknowledged that social issues affect an entire community and a lone wolf grantmaker is not usually as effective as a grantmaker who collaborates with others. There are several ways to collaborate with other grantmakers.

The most visible is a formal collaboration where several grantmakers, sometimes in concert with nonprofits, conceptualize a project and contribute to a single organization, which has been chosen or created for the purpose of executing it. Some of these collaborations may be effective but one must be mindful of the additional overhead they create. The collaboration needs to be managed and there will be issues of leadership and decision making. There may be differing views on the collaboration's effectiveness and how much grant support it should receive and for how long. If the collaboration has been driven by grantmakers, there is a risk that nonprofits have just gone along with it to get the grants that they need. JSF has been involved in a few collaborations and results have been mixed.

There are easier ways to collaborate with other grantmakers. One is to simply make a grant to a program that another grantmaker has created or invested in. JSF has frequently invested in an initiative started and named after another foundation, sometimes years after that foundation has moved on. Often when we are investigating a potential grantee, we find that it is supported by other like-minded foundations. This is a good thing and usually makes us more likely to invest.

Your foundation's strategy should call the tune for its grantmaking. If that leads you to collaborate with other foundations, then so much the better. However, beware of the cost, complexity, and potential inefficiency of formal, managed collaborations.

13. SITE VISITS

There is nothing like being there. In Chapter 6, I said that visiting a potential grantee and getting the feel of the place and the people is an essential part of the grantmaking process. Each site visit will deepen your understanding and your relationship with your grantee partner. Visiting grantee partners and the people they serve gives life to foundation work. Just when we think that we understand it all, we learn something that surprises us.

One of JSF's core grantees is the Florida School for the Deaf and the Blind (FSDB) in St. Augustine. I have been to the campus over a dozen times. One year, FSDB requested $60,000 for a playground, and I remember thinking that a new playground would be a nice thing, but it did not seem very high on the priority scale for educating deaf and blind children. It was a close call, but we deferred to our grantee's judgment and made the grant.

A few months later we made a site visit, and at what we thought was its conclusion, Tanya Rhodes, the then director of development, suggested that we see the playground. I almost made the excuse that we didn't have time. We had another site visit in Jacksonville in the afternoon and a meeting after that. I was hungry and unenthused about visiting a playground. But we did have time and I respected Tanya's judgment. So, I deferred to her suggestion. I am glad that I did.

The playground was a tactile laboratory for blind children to experience the physical world. Imagine a place where children can safely learn the consequences of a misstep or a failure to properly interpret a physical cue. Where a child can stumble or fall and not suffer serious hurt or injury. It was ingenious.

James Crozier, the orientation and mobility instructor, hosted our tour and explained the playground. He is a former classroom teacher and an experienced, accomplished educator. To better explain the importance of the playground for blind students, he told us something that happened years ago when he was teaching grade ten.

James is a baseball fan, and he had a blind student who was absolutely nuts about the game. This kid knew every team, every player and where he came from, batting averages, on base percentages, the win/ loss records of every pitcher, and on and on. This student introduced James to baseball in ways he had never imagined. One day James was working at his desk and the student came into the classroom to see him. While he waited, the student indulged his curiosity by feeling around the top of James's desk. There was a baseball glove and a ball. After extensively and carefully feeling them, the student asked James, "What are these?"

James did not believe that the student did not recognize a baseball and glove. This boy lived and breathed baseball. Surely, he could recognize the basic tools of the game and James urged his student to do so. When he finally understood that his student really did not recognize a baseball and glove, James was stunned. He explained the items in detail, and the next day he took his student to a baseball diamond and around all the bases. He let him feel each one and then took him through the infield and outfield.

To this day James remains amazed and deeply affected by that exchange with his grade ten student, who seemingly knew everything about baseball but could not recognize a ball and glove. For us, James's story was instructive. How much do we really understand our grantee's experience? If our grantee partners can be surprised by what they don't understand, how likely are we to know it all?

I often think about how easy it would have been to decline the grant request for a playground and how easy it would have been to decline the offer to see it. We would never have understood the nature and purpose of this playground and the deeper values behind its purpose. How often have we missed these opportunities and never been the wiser? The lesson for us, and for all grantmakers, is to visit your grantees regularly, listen to them while you are there, think carefully, and act slowly.

8

Leading the Foundation's Investment Process

This chapter uses the theoretical framework that was discussed in Chapter 3 and takes foundation leaders through the practical steps required to lead the foundation's investment process. The objective is for you to "own" the foundations investing and not be a passive observer. Foundation leaders should debate and decide the issues that matter most. This chapter aims to identify those issues and discuss how you should approach them.

CHOOSE AN APPROPRIATE INVESTMENT ADVISER

Choosing the right investment adviser is vital to success. Management of an endowment is a process of delegation. The board delegates to its investment committee, which delegates to one or more professional investors. For smaller foundations, the adviser is usually the person or firm that does the foundation's investing. The adviser has discretion to buy and sell financial products and regularly reports to the foundation. For larger foundations (say $50 million or more) the typical adviser does not buy and sell financial products. It sells advice only, and the investing is done by specialized money managers. Very large and giant foundations often have an in-house investment team and one or more outside advisers. Regardless of your foundation's size or system, the investment adviser is key.

JSF has had three investment advisers over twenty-seven years and each of those was right for the time. Our first adviser did the foundation's investing during the first four years when JSF was getting organized. Our second adviser gave advice to JSF's investment committee, which made the decisions. We were a young foundation and most of us had much to learn. We chose an adviser with a large institutional capacity to provide information and education, in addition to advice. JSF's third manager does not have as much institutional depth but has lower fees and offers a simpler and less expensive approach, which should yield higher net returns.

There is one certainty, however. You will not know which adviser is best for your foundation until you look. With the help of a consultant, JSF looked at the universe of professional investment advisers and issued a request for proposals, which told the prospective investment advisers about JSF and what it wanted. We reviewed the proposals, chose the four best, interviewed the firms that had submitted them, went to the office of our top pick for another interview, and then decided.

Most smaller foundations have a more informal process. I am on the board of a community foundation with assets of about $8 million. We chose an excellent adviser based upon referrals from peers. Smaller foundations can obtain referrals from three or four peer foundations, interview those prospective advisers, get references, and choose the most suitable.

Evaluation Criteria

Regardless of the size of a foundation, the hallmark of a good investment adviser is the willingness to listen and understand your foundation's needs. If your foundation seeks sustainable returns, then your adviser needs to understand and help you fashion an investment policy that is likely to produce them.

Some advisers, particularly large institutional ones, have a difficult time hearing their clients. They tend to push standardized investment policies that follow their institutional approach rather than their client's wishes. If your adviser has difficulty hearing you, move on and keep searching.

OTHER THINGS TO LOOK FOR IN A POTENTIAL ADVISER

- What education do the individuals have? Chartered financial analyst (CFA) is a gold standard, but other credentials may suffice, depending upon experience.

- What is their track record?

- What other foundations do they represent?

- What do their references say?

- Are the people you are dealing with owners, or do they work for a big company? The investment industry attracts bright, ambitious people and the best of these usually work for themselves.

- Avoid friends and friends of friends, even when they are well qualified. Objectivity is vital and friendship makes objectivity impossible.

A good investment adviser may help larger foundations to identify and gain access to investments and managers that may be closed to most investors, such as top-quartile private equity and venture capital funds. Foundations with smaller endowments won't likely invest directly in those asset classes but their advisers are nonetheless important for identifying and gaining access to good investments. For any foundation, a good investment adviser should add value far in excess of its fees.

FORMULATE AN APPROPRIATE INVESTMENT POLICY

The heart of investment policy is asset allocation. In Chapter 3 we saw that asset allocation policy, not brilliant stock picking, is the main determinant of investment returns. There is no ideal allocation policy for all foundations. Your foundation's asset allocation policy should be fashioned according to its unique character and needs.

FORMULATING INVESTMENT POLICY

Elements to consider include the following:
- What are your foundation's aspirations?
- Will it spend its endowment in ten, twenty, or thirty years, or does it intend to span multiple generations?

- Does your foundation have continuing grantee obligations that would make it difficult for it to make smaller grants in a down market?
- What is your foundation's tolerance for volatility?

Foundations with fixed obligations (such as supporting a museum) or those with plans to spend their endowment in less than thirty years will likely value stability over higher long-term returns. They will want a more diversified, defensive asset allocation. Most foundations, however, intend to span multiple generations and need sustainable investment returns. For smaller foundations, the asset allocation policy may be as basic as deciding the split between stocks and bonds.

The Critical Question

The question for leaders of perpetual foundation is this: "What mix of equity and bonds is likely to provide the liquidity we need, the stability we desire, and the sustainable returns we need?"

We have seen that equities are the path to sustainable returns. However, investing your entire endowment in stocks is not wise because your foundation needs liquidity to make grants and pay overhead during down markets. Bonds provide liquidity, but a too heavy allocation to bonds will impair the foundation's ability to earn sustainable returns.

Your foundation's financial adviser can produce model asset allocations that are likely to produce sustainable returns and assist foundation leaders in their discussion. This (investment policy) is a board decision, and good preparation is essential. Board members must understand the issues and the likely consequences of whatever they decide to do.

One further comment about bonds. Ensure that your foundation's bond fund is liquid and can return capital on short notice. During the 2008–9 crash some bond funds unpleasantly surprised foundations with liquidity issues. Also, your foundation should hold no cash except what is necessary to fund its operations for the upcoming few months.

REBALANCE REGULARLY (AT LEAST ONCE A YEAR)

Rebalancing means buying and selling to keep your portfolio in line with your asset allocation. For example, say your foundation has an 85/15 allocation between stocks and bonds. At the end of the year, the stock market is up 20 percent and bonds have declined by 1 percent. Stocks now form a greater percentage of your foundation's portfolio, and you must sell some of them and buy more bonds to restore the 85/15 allocation. This is counterintuitive. Why sell good performing stocks so you can buy poor performing bonds? Your inner voice would tell you not to do it. For that reason, rebalancing should be performed according to a pre-established plan, regardless of investment returns. Reversion to the mean ensures that your foundation will eventually be better off for rebalancing. It is part of the discipline of following your foundation's investment policy.

SUPERVISE YOUR INVESTMENT ADVISER AND/OR MANAGERS

It may seem so far that I am advocating that foundation leaders allocate their assets properly and then do nothing for the long term. I wish it were that easy. Foundation leaders must actively supervise the adviser's activities.

The foundation's investment policy will usually contain a benchmark, which can be used to compare its return to the market return. This is an important tool to better understand your foundation's under- or over-performance. Your foundation should also compare its investment return to other foundations and endowments. Your adviser should regularly provide percentile rankings over different periods of time. Performance over shorter periods (such as months or even two or three years) is not as important as the reasons behind it. Over longer time periods, quartile rankings are extremely important. If your foundation is in the top quartile of its peers over periods of five, ten, or more years, then you have done a fantastic job!

ASK THE RIGHT QUESTIONS

Supervising your foundation's adviser and managers means obtaining and reading regular reports, being prepared for quarterly meetings, and raising questions, such as the following:

- What is foundation investment performance relative to its benchmark and peers' performance over the last three, five, ten years, and more?
- Is the adviser following the investment policy?
- Is the foundation's portfolio up or down more than the market?
- Is there a stock or investment manager that appears to be languishing?
- Is there turnover of the people handling the foundation's account?
- Is the adviser or manager losing key people?

- Has there been a change in ownership of the adviser or manager?

For all these questions ask why, and do not stop asking until you understand the reasons.

Regardless of how foundation leaders feel about the foundation's adviser, they should periodically conduct a review and invite competitors to submit proposals. Just because the relationship has worked well in the past does not mean that it will continue to work well in the future. Foundation leaders should not succumb to inertia. They may like their advisers but must always realize that this is a business relationship, and their interests can never be perfectly aligned. Foundation leaders, not their advisers, are ultimately responsible for the foundation's investment returns.

GET VALUE FOR FEES

The services offered by the financial industry can make foundation investing easy. Just pay the fees and the industry will provide any service you want. Easy investing is not the same as effective investing, however, and it should come as no surprise that high fees are uncorrelated with good investment returns. Your job as a foundation leader is to pay no more fees than necessary and to get value for them. What does this look like?

JSF's recent experience is a lesson on what not to do. In 2019, JSF reviewed the fees it was paying and the value it was getting. JSF had annual investment fees of 1.55 percent. Its portfolio was complex and diversified but its returns relative to its peers' (percentile ranking) had been declining. In short, JSF's investment fees had stealthily increased, and it was not getting value for them.

As a foundation's portfolio becomes more complex it gets more expensive and fees get more difficult to determine. Investment managers each charge a different fee and report investment returns net of fees. The fees charged by private equity and venture capital funds can be particularly difficult to calculate.

QUESTIONS TO ASK YOURSELF ONCE A YEAR

A foundation must regularly calculate its total investment fees and ask itself these questions:

- Are we getting value that justifies these fees?
- Can we get the same value for less?
- Can we get more value somewhere else?

Starting with your investment adviser, you should be getting advice that helps the foundation outperform. Better yet if the adviser's fees are lower than its competitors. If you pay investment managers for active management then you should have an expectation that they will outperform the market. Otherwise, use index funds. Either way, compare fees and choose lower fees where you do not have to sacrifice quality. You cannot escape high fees in private equity and venture capital partnerships. Accept this and get value for them. For private equity and venture capital funds, your foundation should expect first or second quartile performance compared to its peers and net returns of at least 3 percent above public equity market indices.

JSF's remedy for excessive fees was to change its investment adviser, reduce the number of active managers, diversify less, and use more index funds. It still pays high fees because 25 percent of its assets are invested in private equity and venture capital partnerships. The difference is that JSF is getting value. The fees in the rest of its portfolio have been reduced significantly. Every dollar saved in fees accrues to your foundation's endowment and compounds. Review your foundation's investment fees annually. Think about the fees that it is paying and ask yourself, "What would a half percent annual savings in fees add to the endowment over the next twenty years?"

BUILD AND MAINTAIN THE POLITICAL WILL TO STAY THE COURSE

The board must understand and buy into the foundation's investment strategy. This requires leadership of those charged with foundation investing. They must ensure that the entire board understands the foundation's investment asset allocation and is committed to it. It is not a simple matter of presenting an investment policy and getting a motion to approve it. The board must understand what it means and its benefits and drawbacks. If the board knows what it is signing up for and why, then it is less likely to react badly when investing fortunes inevitably reverse. When the market takes a downturn, the board should feel that we're all in this together rather than anger at the people responsible for investing. They should have confidence that the market downturn is temporary, and it is best to stay the course.

Maintaining political will requires a regular flow of information to the board regarding the foundation's investment activities and performance.

The board needs to know how investments are performing and why. It needs to be confident that the people entrusted with investing the foundation's assets know what they are doing and are on the case.

WHAT A MARKET CRASH FEELS LIKE

From September 2007 to March 2009, JSF's endowment shrank by one third. Fear swept through the investment world and was hard to resist. In October 2008 I wrote in my monthly report to the board:

> Last month in Rapid City we seemed to be in the worst days of a crisis in the financial markets. We were told that asset backed loan defaults had caused the most dangerous market situation in living memory. Congress agreed on a plan to avert a market meltdown and the Foundation ended September with annualized losses of fifteen percent and a net asset decline of $24 million year-to-date. Most of us were glad to see the end of September. We could hardly be blamed for hoping that the worst was behind us. As it turns out, the carnage was just beginning. We will not have this month's data from our managers for another few weeks but, judging from the performance of global stock market indices, it looks like we are down fifteen percent in the first ten days of October. Fortunately, the losses are getting smaller. Fifteen percent of $154 million is only $23 million.
>
> Yesterday the markets were up ten percent. We can't possibly predict what's next. All we can do is to "keep our heads (when all about us are losing theirs)" and apply ourselves to our usual work of overseeing the Foundation's investments and managing its Grant Programs.

As it turned out, the downturn continued for another six months. Some of our peers sold a substantial portion of their equity, thinking it was the best way to preserve what they had left. Our biggest issues were liquidity and long-term grant commitments, and we were positioned for these. We had enough bonds to pay our grants and operating expenses for almost three years and did not have to sell equity at depressed prices. As for long-term grant commitments, all our grant agreements contained a "market disaster" provision, which fortunately we did not have to invoke.

Eighteen months of market decline seems like forever and the hardest part was to keep the faith and not sell. Concentrating on the intrinsic value of our equity investments helped as did the knowledge that market values are determined by investor sentiment. The highs of 2007 were a product of irrational exuberance, and the lows of 2009 were created by excessive pessimism. Both were illusions.

In March 2009 most of the investment committee attended Commonfund's annual conference and its message was that stocks were undervalued and would correct upwards. This message was timelier than Commonfund could have known. That month equity markets began a steep and prolonged ascent and by 2010 JSF's portfolio had substantially rebounded. In 2013 recovery was complete. Had it given into the pressure of playing it safe, JSF would have lost money that it could never recover.

COMPOSITION AND ROLE OF THE INVESTMENT COMMITTEE

In small foundations, the foundation board may act as the investment committee. For those with a separate investment committee,

I would suggest that the board chair be a member and, for foundations with staff, the CEO. This committee must have political heft and enjoy the trust of the board. At least one member should be or have been a professional investor. Someone with deep knowledge and experience in the financial markets can explain technical issues and help the committee better understand its investment adviser. If you don't have a professional investor on your board, you should import one to the committee.

Apart from the legal prohibitions against self-dealing (which were discussed in Chapter 4), I caution that your position on the investment committee of a foundation will cause you to be bombarded with investment pitches. I delete several emails a day from people and organizations who want to invest some of the foundation's money. I don't even read them. It is harder to handle when the pitch comes from family or a friend. In that case, I refer them to the foundation's investment adviser. As a courtesy, I call the adviser and alert it that this pitch may be coming their way. The adviser knows that the foundation would never invest with a friend or family member of a board member or staff, and the pitch stops there. The adviser gets to be the villain.

9

Eleven Grants and Lessons Learned

This chapter recounts eleven grants made by JSF at various points during its first thirty years. Four produced few results and had negligible impact; seven are among JSF's most successful grants. Unlike the high-profile grantors and grantees described in Chapter 2, these grants attracted little public notice. This was an advantage. JSF was able to invest, and its grantees were free to act, without public criticism or scrutiny.

I hope that you can relate all these grants to JSF's values, mission, strategy, and vision. Looking at them in retrospect, I understand even more why it is important to follow foundation strategy and the principles of grantmaking. I also realize that we aren't gifted with prophecy or perfect insight. Effective grantmaking does not mean perfect grantmaking. Some of our grants fail, some are partially successful, and some are stellar. The success of many grants depends upon timing, when good people, organizations, and ideas come together, and this is often a matter of luck.

FEW RESULTS, NEGLIGIBLE IMPACT

These are the grants that we learned most from. At the end of each of these stories is an explanation of how our practice has evolved. Grantmaking is an imperfect art, and JSF continues to learn and improve its grantmaking practice.

Internships for Underserved Students (2002–3)

This was a grant for an internship program that recruited underserved students and placed them as interns with investment banking, accounting, and law firms. The program was a perfect fit with JSF's mission. Our grantee partner's goal was to obtain fifty applications and place ten interns. Nine applications were obtained, and only one intern was placed. A third-party evaluator reported that our grantee partner's planning, execution, and overall effort had been less than optimal. Further contact with our grantee partner was unproductive.

The difficulty with this grant was that the internship program was unlike any of our prospective grantee's existing activities. JSF should have asked, "How well does the internship program fit your strategy? What is your capacity to execute it? What do you need most from JSF? Would a capacity-building grant or grants be better than a program to increase the number of interns?" Had we asked these questions (and listened properly to the answers) we might have understood that our grantee had little capacity to carry out the tasks required by this grant.

JSF's mistake was not listening. We loved this program and assumed that it would be a good fit. But it was our grantee partner who had to do the work.

JSF's has changed its grantmaking practice to look beyond the application and objectively question grantee capacity and alignment of interest. For example, JSF was approached by a nonprofit school wanting a scholarship grant for students from a neighboring reservation. The application cited many benefits that would result from bringing Indigenous students to this school and was supported by education officials within the reservation. The scholarship program fit JSF's strategy and we were attracted to it. Staff brought the application to the grant program committee, which questioned the school's capacity and desire to properly execute. JSF referred these questions to the school's senior leaders, who concluded that they did not have the resources or ability to effectively undertake this program.

Online Database for Students with Disabilities (2006)

This was a grant to a nonprofit organization that helped students with disabilities obtain meaningful employment. The nonprofit had a reputation for innovative programming and was led by a smart, energetic CEO. We asked if there was a project that we could fund and were given the opportunity to invest in a new venture with the possibility of a very large impact. Just what we wanted! JSF made a grant to fund the construction of an online database that would connect students with disabilities with prospective employers.

The theory was that employers were becoming increasingly aware of their social obligation to hire people with disabilities and the benefits of doing so. However, it can be difficult. Applicants do not have to disclose a disability and employers are not allowed to ask. However, employers can ask about a prospective employee's ability to do the job. The legal ramifications of asking the wrong questions present a delicate problem, which the online database would solve. It would give employers access to the résumés of thousands of students with disabilities. They could choose the ones that might be suitable and contact them for an interview. Similarly, students with disabilities would have access to potential employers and jobs. The potential to connect qualified students with willing employers seemed enormous.

Our grantee partner executed flawlessly. The database was constructed on time and was well promoted. The grantee partner's other activities, including its annual conference, attracted substantial interest from students and employers. However, the impact of the database did not live up to JSF's hopes. Admittedly, our expectations may have been unrealistic.

The difficulty with this grant was a problem that we did not anticpate. The database did not fit well with the hiring systems of the big, national employers that we were aiming at. Most of them had their own online systems, which would not interface with ours. Highly motivated employees could and did use the database, but it was easier for the others (and for student applicants) to use the company systems. Although this grant did not achieve the impact we had hoped for, I am glad that we made it. We invested in an excellent grantee partner and took a calculated risk.

JSF has learned to be more realistic and is wary of silver bullet solutions to long-standing problems. We are still willing to take risks on new ideas and unproven organizations, but with tempered expectations.

Career Services for Students with Disabilities (2004–7)

This was a multiyear grant to a university to enhance career services and employment outcomes for students with disabilities. The champion of this program had previously worked as an executive in a large public company and knew the business world well. He used his contacts to obtain employment opportunities and had an excellent track record of placing students with disabilities in good jobs. He had created this project and it was to be his capstone. Shortly after we had executed the grant agreement, he was overtaken by ill health and had to retire from the university. The program ran its course but did not produce the expected results.

We were kept well informed by the university and were told when the key person reluctantly made the decision to retire. We were sad for him personally and sorry that he could no longer lead the program.

The difficulty with this grant was JSF not re-examining the university's ability to execute the program without its champion. Had we done so, we might have concluded that it could not succeed and ended it. That would have been a difficult discussion and decision. Instead of facing it, we took the easy way out. We lost sight of the first principle, namely that grant-making is a business and grants are investments. A discussion was necessary to protect our investment and might have surprised us. The university might have been feeling obligated to continue with the program and welcomed its early end. We will never know. Avoiding difficult discussions and decisions invariably leads to ineffectual grantmaking.

JSF has changed its grant agreements to include a condition that its grantee is obliged to advise us if a key person leaves. In that case, there is a discussion regarding the grantee's capacity to continue and the feasibility of doing so.

Youth Entrepreneurship Training (YEP) (2000–3)

This was a program to develop and deliver high school entrepreneurship education to Indigenous youth on reservations in the United States. JSF hired a consultant who reviewed existing programs and literature; surveyed youth, educators, and businesspeople; and convened a planning conference. Initial results showed that no entrepreneurship program existed for Indigenous youth and that there was high interest among students, educators, and business. Based on these findings, we made grants for teachers to be trained in the REAL (Rural Entrepreneurship through Action Learning) Curriculum and launched a one-year pilot in three school districts located in the Pine Ridge and Rosebud reservations of South Dakota. The pilots concluded in May 2003, and after further site visits and consultation, JSF discontinued funding.

What happened?

There were significant challenges beyond the control of JSF. First was high employee turnover in schools. One school had five principals during the one-year pilot of the program. Of the eleven teachers trained in the REAL Curriculum, ten were no longer teaching business a year later. Other priorities, such as the No Child Left Behind federal reform legislation, took focus from elective courses like YEP. A youth entrepreneurship program requires school and community business resources, and there was a lack of both in the Pine Ridge and Rosebud reservations. Finally, most of the YEP students had little financial literacy. They were unfamiliar with the basics of budgeting, banking, and most financial practices.

The difficulty with this grant was that JSF lacked the knowledge and capacity to carry out such an ambitious plan. To have any chance of success it would have required full-time staff, a deeper knowledge of the people and resources of the reservations, and the development of a culturally appropriate curriculum. JSF underestimated the difficulty of executing the YEP program. This was a common mistake in our early grantmaking.

JSF's grantmaking practice has matured. We realize the importance of knowledge and better understand our limitations.

EXCELLENT RESULTS, HIGH IMPACT

These grants also taught us lessons, but they are more remarkable for the grantees that we worked with and the people they served. In these stories, I try to convey a sense of their personas, how much we learned from them, and the satisfaction we got from helping them to succeed.

Scholarships for Students with Disabilities at State University System of Florida (1991 to present)

This program was created by Theodore Johnson, who wanted to establish a perpetual scholarship for people with disabilities. He persuaded the State of Florida to match 50 percent of the foundation's contributions and to manage the program. I don't know the back story, but Mr. Johnson must have been irresistible at age ninety, settling the family fortune on scholarships for young people. The Theodore R. and Vivian M. Johnson Scholarship Act was passed by the Florida Legislature and a perpetual scholarship was created.

When I became CEO in 2001, I was ambivalent about inheriting a perpetual scholarship program. I contacted Lynda Page, who managed the program for the state, and we discussed some ideas to enhance it. Fortunately, she was open to working with us and I began to see the program's advantages. After twenty years, it has become a model partnership among government, higher education, and philanthropy. It is one of our most effective scholarship programs.

The State of Florida and the twelve state universities reap a large benefit compared to the program's cost to them. The state's financial outlay is about $325,000 annually plus the incremental cost of administering the scholarship through its existing management system. The average financial outlay for each of the twelve state universities is $12,000 plus the incremental cost of taking applications and awarding the scholarships to their students through their disability resource centers. The benefit for the state and its universities is a program that produces annual scholarships amounting to $1.3 million, plus support to recipients.

JSF's annual financial outlay is about $800,000. Its status as a permanent funder allows it to accumulate knowledge and build a reputation, which it uses to implement measures that add value to the program. JSF convenes and pays expenses for an annual meeting of the disability resource directors, the state administrator, guest experts, and foundation staff and board members. Different issues affecting the universities and their students are discussed each year, and the conference has become a valued event. JSF also coordinates with some of the state universities to plan events at which scholarship recipients are honored.

Scholarships for students with disabilities are not common and this is one of the few statewide ones. In 2006 this program was recognized nationally by the Association on Higher Education and Disability. The benefits to students go much further than money. They tell us that the support from their disability service centers and the faith shown in them are both fundamental to their success.

This grant taught us the value of partnerships. It is not a large amount of money that makes a scholarship program effective; the money is small compared to the unmet need. What makes *this program work is the partnership among the state, its universities, and the foundation. The basic elements for this partnership can be found anywhere there is higher education, and it can be replicated on almost any scale.*

Scholarships and Capacity Building for Berklee City Music (2000–9)

City Music is a program of Berklee College of Music (Berklee) and was our first foray into grantmaking for underserved students. We were attracted to the idea of using music as a medium to connect with underserved city youth and stumbled into a perfect situation. We learned a lot that helped us to be a better grantmaker in this field. I still marvel at how lucky we were.

Berklee is one of America's great success stories. It was established in Boston by Lawrence Berk in 1945 as a private music school to teach jazz and contemporary music to professional musicians. Today it offers undergraduate and postgraduate degrees in music, theatre, and dance. It is widely acclaimed and has a large international student population; campuses in Boston, New York, and Valencia, Spain; and online music instruction that reaches students from 150 countries.

When we began with Berklee, City Music was a scholarship program that awarded scholarships to underserved Boston youth for a five-week summer performance program in Boston. It also awarded renewable full-tuition scholarships to four of the most promising of the summer performance students. The idea was to help the low-income youth of Boston and, perhaps more important, to obtain their artistic contribution. Curtis Warner, a Berklee alum, was hired to head the program. Curtis was an experienced educator and musician, he knew the city and its youth, and he had a flair for showmanship. He was the perfect person to build City Music.

JSF began by making a grant for four more full-tuition scholarships for underserved students from the City Music program. When we asked Curtis what else we could do, he requested a grant to establish a preparatory school, which would attract children in grades six, seven, and eight. He knew that scholarships were not enough. He wanted to build a program that would impact thousands.

Most of the young people who participated in City Music Preparatory School dreamed of being performers. Being a school of contemporary music—particularly jazz, blues, hip-hop, and rap— gave Berklee credibility in their eyes. The preparatory school does teach music, but it also helps young people to build work habits and self-confidence. The real magic of the preparatory school is that it engages students in a progression that leads toward high school graduation and postsecondary education. A few years later, with a grant from the GMAC Foundation, City Music lowered the preparatory school ages to grades four and five.

In 2004, Roger Brown became Berklee's third president. Roger was another perfect person for the moment. He and his wife, Linda Mason, had enjoyed great success in business. Roger saw the potential in City Music and negotiated a matching-grant agreement with JSF to help Berklee build an endowment for City Music over four years. The agreement challenged Berklee to increase its fundraising for City Music, which, under Roger's leadership, it did exponentially.

Berklee's entrepreneurial approach was not limited to fundraising. Roger and Curtis created the City Music Network, which expanded the program to other cities and countries in partnership with local nonprofits. In 2010, JSF made a multiyear matching grant to the City Music Network to fund scholarships for students from other cities. By 2022, the City Music Network was in forty-seven locations in the United States, Canada, and other countries.

Curtis Warner retired in 2018. He was succeeded by Krystal Banfield, who he had hired over ten years earlier. Like Curtis, she is a musician with impeccable education credentials. Under her leadership, City Music annually serves two thousand students in Boston and over 62,000 students in other City Music Network cities. Roger Brown retired in 2021 and was succeeded by Erica Muhl, a composer and conductor. City Music continues to attract, engage, mentor, and educate underserved youth in Boston and elsewhere, and produces professionals from every discipline, including music, law, and medicine. Four full-time administrators and twelve of Berklee's faculty members, including the dean of Berklee's largest division (performance)—all children of low-income families—have come from City Music.

This grant taught us the rewards of being at the right place at the right time, where good institutions, people, and ideas intersect. JSF's grants were a catalyst for City Music's development and growth and, when these grants were at their peak, JSF was Berklee's largest funder. Today, City Music and Berklee are giants and JSF is small in comparison. City Music also taught us the importance of reaching students in their younger, formative years and making a connection. JSF was able to support and observe the process of mentoring children to help them build work habits, confidence, and a vision of success.

Entrepreneurship and Business Scholarships for Indigenous Peoples (1995 to present)

These were grants to tribal colleges to fund students enrolled in entrepreneurship or business. At the time, tribal colleges were woefully underequipped and underfunded. They worked out of trailers, abandoned buildings, and private homes. We thought that business and entrepreneurship education at tribal colleges would help increase economic activity and the number of jobs on reservations. Initially, JSF made scholarship grants to any tribal college that would take them, but we soon found that we did not have the money or the staff to do them all justice. In 2003, we reduced the number of participating colleges from thirty to ten, and we have kept the number between ten and fifteen since then.

We also help participating colleges to build endowments, which fund scholarships and contribute to the cost of faculty. After the endowment is completed, JSF can exit and move on to serve other colleges. So far, we have helped build nine endowments at tribal and other colleges serving Indigenous students. These colleges now administer and fund business and entrepreneurship scholarships independent of JSF. We have partnered with the American Indian College Fund and Native Forward Scholars Fund to create additional endowments to support business and entrepreneurship students.

Tribal colleges offer great value. Tuition is low, as is the cost of living on reservations. A typical JSF scholarship at a tribal college is $4,000 per year. These colleges are making permanent change, and JSF is proud to have them as partners. Their faculty members are unsung heroes, who work tirelessly, with faith and passion. JSF's program includes an annual convening for representatives of participating colleges, where they can socialize, compare practices, hear guest speakers, discuss new ideas, and offer suggestions to improve the program. JSF makes annual site visits to its college partners and supports related institutions such as the American Indigenous Business Leaders, the American Indian Science and Engineering Society, the American Indian Higher Education Consortium, the First Peoples Fund, and the Native CDFI Network.

Since the 1990s, tribal college facilities have improved dramatically, and many of them have constructed beautiful buildings and campuses. Faculties have improved and students tend to be younger. They have higher expectations and are creating and finding gainful employment on reservations. JSF's scholarship program has contributed to this.

In 2018, JSF commissioned a study of the effect of its scholarships at Oglala Lakota College on the Pine Ridge Reservation in South Dakota. Pine Ridge is one of the poorest counties in the United States and has an unemployment rate of 80 percent. A survey of students who received Johnson Scholarships found that 50 percent of the respondents obtained a bachelor's degree or higher and 20 percent obtained a two-year associate degree. Most of them are employed. Sixty percent of the respondents work in business-related positions for Native and non-Native organizations and 20 percent are self-employed. One JSF scholarship recipient is the Tribal Chairperson at Pine Ridge. The results from this study were particularly welcome because for many years, JSF could find no evidence that its grants were making an impact.

These grants taught us the importance of taking a long view and sticking to our strategy. Education creates an ethic that is passed from one person to another and from one generation to the next. Change takes a long time to observe and JSF's perpetual horizon has helped it to succeed in Indian Country.[124] *Our grantee partners know that our interest is long term, and this resonates with their values and the problems they face. Lack of education and opportunity, and unemployment on reservations have existed for many generations and remediation will take time. Education, particularly business education, is a great investment for grantmakers seeking impact.*

Eye to Eye (2008 to present)

JSF was seeking riskier and potentially more impactful opportunities and Eye to Eye was a perfect fit. Its creators were two recent graduates from Brown University with learning disabilities, who had developed an idea to mentor middle-school children with learning disabilities. The mentoring was delivered by students with learning disabilities, who were organized into chapters, each based on a university campus and supervised by a faculty member. The university students were volunteers and there were four chapters. The dream was to grow this operation and make a meaningful impact.

JSF was new at this, and we asked David Flink, one of the founders, "What is your disability? You are bright and enterprising and have graduated from an Ivy League University." He explained that he had dyslexia and ADHD. He was unable to learn reading when it was taught in his general education classroom, struggled with attention issues, and, most profoundly, struggled with feelings of shame and low self-esteem. It wasn't until he understood his disability, how to use compensatory tools to unleash his potential, and how to advocate for himself, and—most important—found community, that he was able to succeed.

Learning disabilities come in various forms, but David Flink's story is typical. Middle and high school can be a hell on earth for children with learning disabilities. They do not understand language in the same way as their peers, don't learn to read on time, struggle with attention issues, believe that they are stupid, and suffer socially. Many of them bear the shame of this secretly and have a plan for suicide. They need hope. They need to understand their disability, learn how to compensate, and find community. Without help, they are vulnerable to dropping out of school and a life of under- or unemployment or worse.

What sold us on Eye to Eye was that intervention at middle school would make a difference. With insight and compensating strategies, most of these students can graduate, obtain postsecondary education, and obtain meaningful employment. This fit perfectly with our mission and strategy for students with disabilities.

Eye to Eye had small operations, no board, no staff, and little money. After a year of discussions and visits back and forth, JSF made a substantial grant. David Flink had been working out of his apartment in Brooklyn and the grant enabled him to open an office and hire Marcus Soutra. Together they have built a strong and successful organization. Eye to Eye has opened over two hundred mentoring chapters and has added related services such as teacher training. David Flink has written a book, *Thinking Differently*, and he was recognized as a CNN hero in 2021.[125] Eye to Eye is run by and for people with learning differences.

Eye to Eye is well known and respected in its field and has attracted widespread philanthropic support. Flink and Soutra have turned out to be excellent businesspeople, and Eye to Eye is financially stable and responsibly managed. It no longer needs large-scale support from JSF. JSF still makes occasional grants to Eye to Eye because its model allows it to reach thousands of young people every year at a fraction of the cost of scholarships.

This grant taught us the rewards of occasionally betting on people who have a good idea but few resources and no track record. JSF mitigated its risk by due diligence. We got to know David Flink and the Eye to Eye concept and we helped him to mold his thinking for an organization, board, and operations. David proved to be a gifted leader and the Eye to Eye concept worked well. The impact of JSF's investment in Eye to Eye far outweighs the inevitable failures of taking risks in grantmaking. JSF's first grant catalyzed Eye to Eye and helped it to become what it is today.

Machen Florida Opportunity Scholarships (2011–15; 2020 to present)

University of Florida (UF) is among the largest and most affluent state universities in the United States. Its annual budget is almost $4 billion, the market value of its endowment is over $2 billion, and its student population is over 60,000. It is hardly the place where JSF would invest and this is what I told Margaret Atherton, executive director of development of corporate and foundation relations, when she called and suggested that we meet. I did not want to waste her time.

In my office a few weeks later Margaret listened patiently as I explained JSF's mission to assist people in financial need, which usually meant minority students. Like everyone else, I knew of UF's prowess in college football and basketball, so I also told her that JSF was not interested in funding these or any other sports. When I finished talking, she explained that UF's student population was among the most racially diverse in the United States. As for the football and basketball programs, they are net contributors and need no funding from JSF. Margaret was well aware of JSF's mission and strategy and had come to discuss a new scholarship program, which she felt certain would be of interest.

The Machen Florida Opportunity Scholarship (MFOS) was created for first-generation students, students of parents who had not graduated from college. To be eligible, students must first be admitted to UF, which has the highest admission standards of any of the Florida state universities. The average annual family income of MFOS scholarship recipients is less than $24,000 per year.

MFOS is directly on point with JSF's mission and strategy, and despite our initial skepticism, we went to Gainesville and were introduced to students and to the program's then-director, Leslie Pendleton. She and her staff had constructed a UF community support system, which includes academic counselors, personal counselors, and student mentors. Students from families with low incomes are particularly susceptible to *imposter syndrome*, which causes them to interpret the usual trials and tribulations of acclimatizing to university life as confirmation that they do not belong. The natural response is to drop out. The support system anticipates this and helps students realize that it is okay to ask for help. This fits perfectly with JSF's research and experience.[126] Students from families with low incomes perform better when they are placed among students from affluent families. They learn that they are entitled to help and that they should ask for it when they need it.

At the beginning, UF took steps to ensure anonymity of MFOS scholars so that they would not feel stigmatized. But MFOS students do not want anonymity. They are proud of where they come from and who they are. They are scholars. This is the power of the program. MFOS students see themselves as intelligent, industrious men and women who add value to UF. We have met many of these students and they are remarkable. They exude maturity, enthusiasm, and confidence. They know what they want and how to get it.

JSF has made two multiyear grants to MFOS. The first began in 2012 and was a matching grant of four dollars from UF donors for every one dollar from JSF. The matching funds had to be put to the same use (MFOS), but JSF did not request recognition for its grant or the matching funds. In 2019, UF wanted to increase the number of Machen Scholars and approached JSF again. We made a further grant with a similar matching requirement. Matching leverages JSF's grant and assists UF's fundraising.

MFOS has become a darling of staff and faculty, who donate time and money to the scholarship. The cost of MFOS's extensive support services is funded by UF's budget and not from the scholarship fund.

Machen scholars compose over 5 percent of every year's freshmen class. Student testimonials stress two things. First, MFOS makes UF accessible to students who would not otherwise be able to attend. Second, Machen Scholars are not under heavy pressure to work while attending and can graduate debt free. Retention and graduation rates for MFOS students surpass UF, state, and national averages, which has helped UF to become the fifth-highest ranked state university in the United States. Every year MFOS gives a full financial ride to 1,600 students and has built a system of nonmonetary support that assures their success. Imagine the impact!

As the name suggests MFOS was championed by Bernie Machen. He became UF's eleventh president in 2004 and began to build institutional support for his vision to recruit students from families with low income. He created the Florida Opportunities Scholarship[127] and donated a substantial portion of his salary to it. President Machen retired in 2015 and is still active in MFOS and raising money for it.

This grant taught us that good investment opportunities depend as much on the situation as the institutions. In this partnership JSF is the small fry and UF the giant. However, MFOS is directly on point with JSF's mission and strategy. President Machen's vision required private grant money and JSF was able to have a significant impact because its money was matched by other potential donors. This speaks to the benefit of following a strategy for decades. JSF has built a reputation for helping to build scholarship programs for students with financial need, and like-minded donors are more likely to invest when they see that we have invested. This grant also highlights the value of a good development officer. It was Margaret Atherton who apprised us of this opportunity and explained why it was such a good fit.

Johnson Scholars (2009 to present)

The idea for this program came from another foundation, which was delivering a similar program in two other states, where it was a home run with students, schools, and governments. We decided to adapt it and considered several locations before settling on Palm Beach County. JSF's offices are in West Palm Beach, and we reasoned that a program close to home would be a better fit. Despite Palm Beach County's remarkable wealth, 12 percent of its population lives in poverty. Its student population is 200,000, which makes it the tenth-largest school district in the United States.

We approached the school board and offered funding for student support and scholarships if the board would build and deliver the program. The aim of the program is to mentor students with good potential and poor prospects so that they can graduate from high school and go to college. The program began at five of the poorest high schools in the county and works like this. At the end of grade eight, students (with support from their families) apply to the school for admission into the program. To be eligible they must qualify for the school district's free and reduced lunch program. Fifteen students are accepted and placed in a cohort beginning in grade nine and continuing until their senior year.

The next year, the school chooses another grade nine cohort. Each year, from grade nine to twelve inclusive, has a cohort of Johnson Scholars. The school has a college readiness club comprising the Johnson Scholars from all grades. The club meets monthly, and students also attend lunch and after-school meetings. The goal is to equip these students—academically, emotionally, and socially— to take advantage of the opportunity to attend college. The work in the schools is done by school-based coordinators, supplemented by AmeriCorps volunteer workers. Students who complete the program and qualify for college admission are offered scholarships, which are renewable for up to four years. The four-year scholarship is the carrot, but most of the value of this program is imparted in the schools.

After the Johnson Scholars program was underway, JSF learned of a similar program in Palm Beach, Take Stock in Children (Take Stock). It has an excellent statewide mentoring and scholarship program that is similar to the Johnson Scholars, except that support services are delivered outside of the school system. Take Stock has access to lower-cost scholarships through the Florida Prepaid College Foundation and we began buying prepaid scholarships from Take Stock for use by Johnson Scholars. In 2016, Take Stock Palm Beach, the school system, and JSF executed a partnership agreement that joined the two programs, and JSF committed to a series of grants to support their work.

The combined program is now delivered in eleven schools and provides service to five hundred students, who are likely to graduate from school and attend college. Last year's 125 graduates received scholarships of $1.2 million from the Johnson Scholars/Take Stock program and other universities across the state of Florida. Eleven of them were accepted by UF and awarded Machen Florida Opportunity Scholarships.

Johnson Scholars is based on a good idea, but it was people who made it a great program. First among those is Wanda Kirby, who ran the program for its first twelve years. Nancy Stellway is the executive director of Take Stock in Children Palm Beach. She was able to envision a collaboration among the school board, Take Stock, and JSF and worked hard to make it happen. Gbolade (Bo) George succeeded Wanda as the school system's leader of the Johnson Scholars/Take

Stock program. He, Wanda, and Nancy have provided continuous, skilled, and heartfelt leadership. I suggested to Wanda that the real secret to this program's success was the faith and belief that it placed in students. She agreed that this was important but also pointed out the importance of the structure provided by the program. It provides boundaries for students and sets expectations and consequences, which they need.

Wanda also emphasized the importance of JSF's involvement and support. JSF meets regularly with program leaders and gives feedback and support for new ideas. She and her colleagues know that this is JSF's home program, and they want to meet our expectations. JSF shows up at each school's annual graduation ceremony and at special events when requested. The students' status as Johnson Scholars is important to them, and they always welcome an appearance by the foundation.

This grant taught us the value of other people's ideas and resources. The template for this program came from the ECMC Foundation, which was happy to help us replicate it. Take Stock had unique access to lower-cost scholarships and a similar mentoring program. Merging the two programs benefited the organizations and the students they serve. This is not a competition; we exist to help students. Another lesson from this grant is the importance of showing up for grantees and the students they serve. Foundations sometimes underestimate the effect that they have on others. Showing up for grantees makes the people doing the work feel valued and encouraged. The people that they serve—in this case, students—get to see the human face of the foundation and to meet and talk with the people who believe in them. This is one of our favorite things to do and breathes life into the foundation's relationships with grantees and students.

MBA in American Indian Entrepreneurship (2000–22)

My predecessor, Ted Johnson, Jr., came up with the idea of an MBA in American Indian Entrepreneurship for business faculty at tribal colleges. It would be structured to allow faculty members to study at distance during the fall, winter, and spring (thus allowing them to teach) and then attend classes on campus during the summer. He and I shopped the idea at several universities and settled on Gonzaga University in Spokane, Washington, as best able to develop and deliver it.

We were convinced to choose Gonzaga during a meeting with its president, Father Robert Spitzer, and its dean of business, Clarence (Bud) Barnes. Father Spitzer explained that the original purpose of Gonzaga was to educate Native Americans. The university had gotten away from that purpose, and this would help it to get back to its mission, an opportunity Gonzaga badly wanted. This was an honest admission and made an impression on us.

Bud Barnes was equally as persuasive. He told us that Gonzaga's MBA program was rated in the top 25 percent of the country, and he envisioned an MBA in American Indian Entrepreneurship that had the same standards. Gonzaga could develop an appropriate curriculum and provide on-campus housing for students and their immediate families.

JSF agreed to pay Gonzaga to develop the curriculum and pay all expenses for a minimum of six students per year, even if Gonzaga's enrollment was below that number. It was a gamble. We had no idea how many qualified applicants the program would attract. Some tribal colleges did not support it because Gonzaga was too far away and did not have many Indigenous students or faculty members.

In summer 2001, the program's first cohort of students began classes. They were watched closely by Gonzaga, by JSF, and by the tribal colleges that employed them. One of the students could not keep up with the others. Her classmates stood with her and informed Gonzaga that if she were dismissed from the program, they would not continue. She unselfishly defused the situation by withdrawing voluntarily and urging her classmates to continue. The remaining members of the first cohort stayed with the program, flourished, and graduated on schedule.

After the first year, Gonzaga recommended that the program not be restricted to tribal college faculty. JSF agreed and it was opened to all enrolled members of recognized tribes in the United States and to members of Canadian bands. Even with this change it was difficult to attract six qualified candidates every year. Gonzaga redoubled its recruiting efforts. Stacey Chatman, Gonzaga's student coordinator for this program, travelled around the United States telling prospective students about the program and the scholarship and persuading them to apply. Stacey was also on campus to greet them, help them get acclimatized, and support them as they made their journey. JSF used its tribal college contacts to advertise the program and advocated for it wherever it could. Gradually, the program built a reputation and earned the trust of Indigenous students. Recruiting became easier.

In 2013, JSF commissioned an evaluation[128] from First Nations Development Institute. The report concluded that alumni from the MBA AIE program are helping tribal governments succeed and promoting economic development on reservations. It stated that the program "is successfully supporting the next generation of American Indian leaders . . . to guide community economic change for years to come in Indian Country." The program was also the subject of a paper by Dr. Daniel Stewart and Dr. Molly Pepper, published in 2011 in the *Journal of Management Education*.[129] The paper analyzes the elements that make it successful and describes the impact of its graduates on their communities.

As of 2022, there are eighty-four graduates from this program and they have become tribal college presidents, business and nonprofit leaders, and policymakers. US News and World Report[130] ranks the MBA AIE program fourteenth in the United States in the entrepreneurship specialty category. JSF and Gonzaga have built an endowment, which will provide scholarship support to future Indigenous MBA students.

As impressive as the above sounds, the real impact is best seen through the eyes of a student and graduate of the program.

Angelique Albert is Salish Kootenai, from the Flathead Reservation in Montana, and is the CEO of Native Forward Scholars Fund, the largest provider of scholarships to Indigenous students in the United States. In her first five years, she has increased the number of staff from sixteen to thirty-one and annual revenues from $4 million to $14 million ($34 million if you count last year's grant from MacKenzie Scott). Native Forward has awarded scholarships of $350 million to Native American students.

Angelique obtained an MBA in American Indian Entrepreneurship from Gonzaga in 2014. She and the other graduates of this program are part of a network of high-level Native American executives and educators all over Indian Country and corporate America. She regards them as family, even the ones that she has not met. They are bonded; they know the struggles to get through the program and complete the degree.

Angelique's reason for applying to the Gonzaga program was to position herself for better opportunities. By the time she graduated, it was no longer about her. She wanted to do something with her education that would help Native people.

Angelique is using her education to help empower Native students. There is still much to do. Native American students do not get a proportionate share of philanthropic dollars and Angelique is committed to the cause of obtaining it. Her vision is the same level of financial support for Native students as other students in the United States. They deserve nothing less.

When I think of Angelique and her MBA colleagues, I am struck by three things. First, Native Americans are a relatively small community, and this gives JSF an opportunity to make a greater impact. The Gonzaga MBA offered an opportunity to Native Americans that did not exist. The network of high-powered Native American MBAs makes a permanent difference, and that difference will continue to grow with the graduation of each new cohort of students.

Second, the need is great. Besides Native Forward and the American Indian College Fund there are few scholarship programs available to Indigenous students. The scholarships provided by JSF—and others— have helped students to attend and graduate from college, and those students have used their education to improve their communities.

Third, JSF aspires to be a perpetual foundation and its mission to Indigenous Peoples is permanent. There has been a lot of progress in the last thirty years, but there is still much to do. Many of the reservations still have deep poverty and upwards of 80 percent unemployment. It will take many years for these communities to reach a reasonable level of prosperity and well-being. Philanthropic support from JSF and other foundations will play an important role.

This grant taught us the value of taking a risk on a new idea and sticking with it, even when it is difficult and doesn't seem to be working. It also demonstrated the importance of choosing the right grantee partner. Gonzaga's commitment and execution were extraordinary, and I doubt that any other institution would have succeeded as it did. We also learned that unintended consequences can be good. The plan was to help tribal colleges by offering this program exclusively to their business faculty members. Difficulties in recruiting students made us open the program to all qualified Indigenous students and this has expanded its impact beyond anything we could have imagined.

Parting Thoughts

In the preceding chapters, I have described the essentials of philanthropic practice, its value, and the joy and satisfaction that it brings. I would like to close with some parting thoughts on the future of philanthropy and its place in our society. I do this because you may encounter people who try to delegitimize what you do, people who say that grantmakers are privileged elites that get big tax breaks and don't know or care about today's real problems. These statements are inaccurate but nonetheless dangerous. Philanthropy is not well understood.

A few years ago, I heard Anand Giridharadas speak about his new book, *Winners Take All: The Elite Charade of Changing the World*.[131] The book paints a gloomy picture of economic disparity in American society and describes philanthropists as people who pretend to remedy social problems (that they had a big hand in creating), when their real agenda is to preserve their alpha status:

The only thing better than controlling money and power is to control the efforts to question the distribution of money and power. The only thing better than being a fox is being a fox asked to watch over hens . . . we must decide whether . . . we are willing to allow democratic purpose to be usurped by private actors who often genuinely aspire to improve things but, first things first, seek to protect themselves.[132]

Winners Take All was a smash hit and received favorable reviews from the *New York Times, Washington Post,* and the *Economist,* to name a few. It was as if Giridharadas had pulled back the curtain and revealed the real secret behind philanthropy. Giridharadas's characterization of philanthropy as an "elite charade" has a conspiratorial ring and has struck a populist chord. The book is lively and provocative, and the examples cited contain more than a grain of truth. The basic arguments, however—that philanthropy is a charade perpetrated by elites whose primary interest is to remain in control and that it is undemocratic—do not bear up under scrutiny.

Let's look at the "elite charade" argument and see how it fits with what we know of practicing philanthropists. I wrote about two founding giants of modern philanthropy, John D. Rockefeller and Andrew Carnegie, in Chapter 3 but not about their business careers. It is safe to say that both were self-made, hard-driving businesspeople who, subject to the laws of the land, made as much money as they could. I doubt that anyone would seriously contend that they caused the inequalities of their time. The worst that can be said is that they participated, very successfully, in a system that tolerated too much economic disparity.

Ask yourselves whether it makes sense to think that Carnegie and Rockefeller were engaged in a charade, whether public libraries and medical research were cover for their real agenda to stay in control. How about two modern equivalents, Bill and Melinda Gates? And Warren Buffett's pledging his $100 billion fortune to philanthropy? If this is an act, who are they trying to impress? Why? Would they really donate almost all their money and something infinitely more precious, their time, to a philanthropic mission if they desired above all to maintain their positions atop the economic pyramid?

The idea that foundation leaders are a class of elites (with a cohesive socioeconomic philosophy and agenda) is contrary to everything that I know about philanthropy. The founders of JSF gave their fortune to a foundation because they wanted to help people to empower themselves through education. The present board members of JSF are motivated by that same desire, not by their personal opinions about the status quo. Ask yourself, what do you care about? Your foundation's philanthropic mission or protecting your elite status?

Let's look at the second argument, that democratically elected governments, not philanthropy, should set the agenda for social reform. That sounds good at first blush. Shouldn't our priorities be chosen by elected leaders and not by self-appointed saviors? Look beyond the rhetoric and examine the assumption on which this statement is based, namely that we must choose between philanthropy and democracy. This assumption is false. Philanthropy does not usurp or diminish government policy. It operates at the margins and competes in the marketplace of solutions. Philanthropy may act as a catalyst for change and help to inform government policy, but it does not replace it. It is fallacious to equate philanthropy and government policy and offer a choice of either/or.

We live in a free society where philanthropy, volunteerism, and independent nonprofit organizations are encouraged. Tax deductions are the most tangible form of encouragement. The government gives us a choice. We can keep our money and pay tax on it or donate it and pay less tax. The money donated is always more than the tax, and the tax break is a recognition that philanthropy is good for society. This recognition is what is at stake. If the negativity about philanthropy prevails, tax policy will change, and philanthropy will wither on the vine.

It is up to us to make the case for philanthropy. We can each do this by practicing philanthropy as impeccably as we can, and I hope that this book will help. We can also speak up about the work of our foundation, so that the public will understand its value. By advocating for philanthropy, foundation leaders are protecting their interests, not as selfish elites but as people who understand the opportunity they have been given: to improve society through free and independent grant-making. This opportunity is unique and has proven its value over time. It is worth preserving.

As noted in Mr. Martin's foreword, we are amid the largest transfer of generational wealth in history. What will it look like? How will philanthropy affect the issues of our time? What versions of Rockefeller's medical research or Carnegie's public libraries will emerge? We can be optimistic. Philanthropy continues to grow, to be better supported, and to be practiced more effectively.

Thank you for taking the time to read this book. I hope that you have found it helpful, and I wish you every success in your foundation practice. May you make your mark on philanthropy's future and enjoy yourself in the process.

Acknowledgements

I give heartfelt thanks to David Blaikie, Lorne Brett, Hugh Brown, Phil Buchanan, Bill Corwin, Mike Doyle, Lady Hereford, King Jordan, Bobby Krause, Mike Miller, Maridel Moulton, Barbara Stanley, and David and Fraser Wells, who were patient and generous in giving their time and energy to read and improve this manuscript. Thank you to Caitlin Schryver for her excellent research and advice on the investment chapters, and to Richard Morrison and Prime Buchholz for providing valuable data and information. Thanks also to my superb, steadfast editor, Eleanor Gasparik, who made me work harder and edit more. All of you helped to make this a better book. I am grateful to the board of JSF for its support and encouragement. The mistakes in this book belong to me only, as do the opinions and statements.

My special thanks go to the Right Honourable Paul Martin, who encouraged me to write this book and has been a constant source of inspiration and help.

Suggested Reading

Grantmaking

Brest, Paul, and Hal Harvey. *Money Well Spent: A Strategic Plan for Smart Philanthropy*. 2nd ed. Stanford: Stanford University Press, 2018.

Buchanan, Phil. *Giving Done Right: Effective Philanthropy and Making Every Dollar Count*. New York: PublicAffairs, 2019.

Chernow, Ron. *Titan: The Life of John D. Rockefeller, Sr.* New York: Random House, 1998.

Fleishman, Joel. *The Foundation: A Great American Secret*. New York: PublicAffairs, 2007.

Fleishman, Joel, Scott Kohler, and Steven Schindler. *Casebook for the Foundation: A Great American Secret*. New York: PublicAffairs, 2007.

Frumkin, Peter. *The Essence of Strategic Giving: A Practical Guide for Donors and Fundraisers*. Chicago: The University of Chicago Press, 2010.

Setterberg, Fred, and Bill Sommerville. *Grassroots Philanthropy: Field Notes of a Maverick Grantmaker*. Berkeley: Heyday Books, 2008.

Tierney, Thomas, and Joel Fleishman. *Give Smart: Philanthropy that Gets Results*. New York: PublicAffairs, 2011.

Investing

Bogle, John. *The Little Book of Common Sense Investing: The Only Way to Guarantee Your Fair Share of Stock Market Returns*. 10th ed. New York: John Wiley and Sons, 2017.

Buffett, Warren. *Berkshire Hathaway Inc. Shareholder Letters: 1972 to 2022*. Berkshire Hathaway. https://www.berkshirehathaway.com/letters/letters.html.

Siegel, Jeremy. *Stocks for the Long Run*. 6th ed. New York: McGraw Hill, 2023.

Governance

Chait, Richard P., William P. Ryan, and Barbara E. Taylor. *Governance as Leadership: Reframing the Work of Nonprofit Boards*. New York: John Wiley and Sons, 2005.

Collins, James. *Good to Great*. New York: Harper Collins, 2001.

Collins, James, and Jerry Porras. *Built to Last: Successful Habits of Visionary Companies*. New York: Harper Collins, 1994.

Trower, Cathy. *The Practitioners' Guide to Governance as Leadership: Building High-Performing Nonprofit Boards*. San Francisco: Jossey Bass, 2013.

Endnotes

1. "U.S. Social Sector," Candid, accessed June 15, 2023, https://candid.org/explore-issues/us-social-sector/organizations.

2. "Canadian Foundation Facts," Philanthropic Foundations Canada, accessed June 15, 2023, https://pfc.ca/canadian-foundation-facts/.

3. "U.S. Social Sector," Candid; and "Canadian Foundation Facts," Philanthropic Foundations Canada.

4. Based upon IRS data. This information was drawn from 2020 990PF data on the IRS website: "SOI Tax Stats—Annual Extract of Tax-Exempt Organization Financial Data," Internal Revenue Service, last modified April 4, 2013, https://www.irs.gov/statistics/soi-tax-stats-annual-extract-of-tax-exempt-organization-financial-data.

5. Malcolm Gladwell, *Outliers: The Story of Success* (Boston: Little, Brown, 2009).

6. Ron Chernow, *Titan: The Life of John D. Rockefeller, Sr.* (New York: Random House, 1998).

7. From inception until January 31, 2023, JSF's annual nominal return was 9.4 percent, and its real (after inflation) return since inception was 6.9 percent. This puts it in the top quartile of foundation investment performance.

8. Peter Frumkin, *The Essence of Strategic Giving* (Chicago: University of Chicago Press, 2006), viii.

9. "John Rockefeller Sr.," Philanthropy Roundtable, accessed July 7, 2023, https://www.philanthropyroundtable.org/hall-of-fame/john-rockefeller-sr/.

10. Chernow, *Titan*, 445–47. In Rockefeller's early days in Cleveland, Fred Backus had been a bookkeeper in his office and taught Sunday School at his church. Backus later started a small lubricating company, not a particularly profitable one, and died at the age of forty. When Standard Oil approached "the Widow Backus" about buying her late husband's business, she insisted on dealing with Mr. Rockefeller. This was a piffling transaction for Standard Oil, but Rockefeller personally intervened and saw that Mrs. Backus was generously treated. When she later complained publicly that she had been swindled, Rockefeller offered to restore the business to her for the return of the money. Chernow's conclusion is worth quoting: "By investing her proceeds in Cleveland real estate instead, Backus, far from being reduced to filth and misery, became an extremely rich woman . . . she was worth $300,000 at her death. Nevertheless, the supposed theft of Backus Oil became an idee fixe, and she dredged up the story for anyone who cared to listen. The notion of Rockefeller gleefully ruining a poor widow was such a good story, with so fine a Dickensian ring, that gullible reporters gave it fresh circulation for many years."

11. Karl Zinsmeister, *The Almanac of American Philanthropy* (Washington, DC: Philanthropy Roundtable, 2016), 205.

12. Chernow, *Titan*, 321.

13. Chernow, *Titan*, 341.

14. The IRS website describes qualifying distributions as "any amount (including program-related investments) paid to accomplish religious, charitable, scientific, literary, or other public purposes" but do not include contributions to organizations controlled by the contributing foundation or by one or more disqualified persons ("Qualifying Distributions—In General," Internal Revenue Service, last modified January 9, 2023, https://www.irs.gov/charities-non-profits/private-foundations/qualifying-distributions-in-general). In Canada, the CRA website defines qualified donees as "organizations that can issue official donation receipts for gifts they receive from individuals and corporations" ("Qualified Donees," Canada Revenue Agency, last modified January 11, 2017, https://www.canada.ca/en/revenue-agency/services/charities-giving/charities/policies-guidance/qualified-donees.html).

15. This is taken from my notes after a keynote address by Dr. Raymond at a conference I attended in 2006. While researching Dr. Raymond for the purpose of

this citation, I saw that she has coined the invocation "Immerse Yourself," which I use later in this chapter. We came to the same phrase independently, but she said it first. Dr. Raymond has had a distinguished career as a writer and leader in philanthropy and nonprofit worlds and is still active.

16. Bill Somerville, *Grassroots Philanthropy: Fieldnotes from a Maverick Grantmaker* (Berkley: Heydey, 2008), chap. 6, location 1308, Kindle.

17. Andrew Carnegie, "The Gospel of Wealth," *North American Review*, 1889.

18. Ellie Buteau, Naomi Orensten, and Charis Loh, *The Future of Foundation Philanthropy: The CEO Perspective* (Cambridge, MA: Center for Effective Philanthropy, 2016), https://cep.org/portfolio/future-foundation -philanthropy-ceo-perspective/.

19. Kevin Bolduc, Ellie Buteau, Greg Laughlin, Ron Ragin, and Judith A. Ross, *Foundation Strategy: Beyond the Rhetoric* (Cambridge, MA: Center for Effective Philanthropy, 2007), https://cep.org/portfolio/beyond-the-rhetoric -foundation-strategy-2/.

20. Adam Grant, *Think Again* (New York: Random House, 2021).

21. Grant, 214.

22. Grant, 210.

23. *New Oxford American Dictionary*, 3rd ed. (New York: Oxford University Press, 2010).

24. For a contrary view, see Phil Buchanan, *Giving Done Right* (New York: PublicAffairs, 2019), 36–38.

25. People unfamiliar with grantmaking tend to fixate on the grant transaction itself and not the issues that the grant attempts to address. This is reflected in most media accounts of grantmaking, which tend to focus on the amount and the "generosity" of the donor. Very few of those accounts provide any description or analysis of the strategy behind those grants.

26. Somerville, *Grassroots Philanthropy*, location 1840.

27. JSF has one program that makes awards directly to students. Permission for this was required from the US Internal Revenue Service (IRS) and granted on condition that an arm's length third party be retained to receive and evaluate applications and make the awards.

28. Susan Stamberg, "How Andrew Carnegie Turned His Fortune into a Library Legacy," *NPR*, August 1, 2013, https://www.npr.org/2013/08/01/207272849/how-andrew-carnegie-turned-his-fortune-into-a-library-legacy.

29. David Nasaw, *Andrew Carnegie* (New York: Penguin Books, 2006).

30. Carnegie, *Gospel of Wealth*, 20.

31. Carnegie, 13.

32. Carnegie, 35.

33. Carnegie, 25.

34. Vartan Gregorian, "Libraries and Andrew Carnegie's Challenge," *Report of the President 1998* (New York: Carnegie Foundation, 1998), 23.

35. Carnegie, *Gospel of Wealth*, 589.

36. "Carnegie's Canadian Libraries," Canada's Historic Places, accessed June 16, 2023, https://www.historicplaces.ca/en/pages/34_carnegie.aspx.

37. Carnegie, *Gospel of Wealth*, 604, fn 30.

38. Carnegie, 606.

39. Carnegie, 607.

40. Carnegie, 609.

41. Carnegie, 607.

42. I have relied heavily upon three sources: Kenn Harper, *Minik: The New York Eskimo* (Hanover, NH: Steerforth Press, 2017; Kelly Lara Lankford, "Home Only Long Enough: Arctic Explorer Robert E. Peary, American Science, Nationalism, and Philanthropy, 1886–1908" (PhD diss., University of Oklahoma, 2003), https://hdl.handle.net/11244/603; and Penny Petrone, ed., *Northern Voices* (Toronto: University of Toronto Press, 1988).

43. Harper, *Minik*, 234.

44. Accounts of the amount vary from $40,000 to $50,000 (Harper, *Minik*). Either way, that is over $1 million today.

45. Harper, *Minik*, 30.

46. Harper, 229.

47. Petrone, 80–84.

48. Most of the information for this story comes from Steven Schindler, "Case 23: Preventing Crashes on America's Highways," in *Casebook for the Foundation: A Great American Secret*, Joel Fleishman, Scott Kohler, and Steven Schindler (New York: PublicAffairs, 2007).

49. Schindler, 66.

50. Schindler, 67.

51. Schindler, 67.

52. Schindler, 69.

53. Commonfund, *A Common Vision: Working in Partnership for the Benefit of All*, 1971–1996 (Connecticut: Commonfund, 1996), 7.

54. George F. Keane, "A Brief History: A Dream Fulfilled," in *A Common Vision: Working in Partnership for the Benefit of All*, 1971–1996 (Connecticut: Commonfund, 1996), 20.

55. Keane, 26.

56. Most of this narrative comes from an interview and correspondence with Brian Mullaney.

57. Reed Abelson with Elisabeth Rosenthal, "Charges of Shoddy Practices Taint Gifts of Plastic Surgery," *New York Times*, November 24, 1999, https://www.nytimes.com/1999/11/24/world/charges-of-shoddy-practices-taint-gifts-of-plastic-surgery.html.

58. Elisabeth Rosenthal with Reed Abelson, "Whirlwind of Facial Surgery by Foreigners Upsets China," *New York Times*, November 25, 1999, https://www.nytimes.com/1999/11/25/world/whirlwind-of-facial-surgery-by-foreigners-upsets-china.html.

59. Abelson with Rosenthal, "Charges of Shoddy Practices."

60. As an aside, it turned out that local surgeons needed less training than Smile Train anticipated. The surgeons of most developing countries are skilled at cleft surgery. Perhaps more important than training surgeons is the money and systemic improvements in surgical practice that Smile Train has provided.

61. The one and a half million number is from Smile Train's website. The Operation Smile number, 135,000, is from Elizabeth Simpson, "'Smile' Charity Leaders in midst of Decade-Long Feud," *Virginian-Pilot*, December 20, 2009, 3.

62. "Global Outreach," Operation Smile, accessed July 7, 2023, https://www.opera-tionsmile.org/global-outreach.

63. "Donate Now and Change a Child's Life Forever," Smile Train, accessed June 18, 2023, https://donate.smiletrain.org/givenow.

64. "Smile Train Audit Report 2019," Smile Train, accessed June 18, 2023, https://www.smiletrain.org/sites/default/files/2021-01/smile-train-audit-report-fy19.pdf. The statement also shows a healthy surplus in income over expenses.

65. "Stronger, Smaller High Schools to Help Thousands of Oregon Students," Bill & Melinda Gates Foundation, accessed June 18, 2023, https://www.gatesfoundation.org/ideas/media-center/press-releases/2003/04/oregon-small-schools-initiative.

66. Jack Schneider, "Small Schools: The Edu-Reform Failure That Wasn't," *EducationWeek*, February 9, 2016, https://www.edweek.org/leadership/opinion-small-schools-the-edu-reform-failure-that-wasnt/2016/02.

67. Schneider, 4.

68. Chernow, *Titan*, 309–13.

69. Chernow, 470.

70. M. S. Kaplan, "Dr. Flexner's Experiment," *Rockefeller University Research Profiles*, Book 30 (New York: Rockefeller University, 1987), https://digitalcommons.rockefeller.edu/research_profiles/30.

71. Chernow, *Titan*, 471.

72. James Thomas Flexner, *An American Saga* (Boston: Little, Brown, 1984).

73. Flexner, 439.

74. George W. Corner, *A History of the Rockefeller Institute* (New York: Rockefeller Institute Press, 1964), 33.

75. Chernow, *Titan*, 473.

76. Flexner, *An American Saga*, 359.

77. Flexner, 362.

78. Chernow, *Titan*, 472.

79. Kaplan, "Dr. Flexner's Experiment," 3.

80. Kaplan, 4.

81. Kaplan, 4.

82. Kaplan, 5.

83. J. S. Billings, "Cerebrospinal Meningitis in New York City during 1904 and 1905," *Journal of American Medicine* 46, no. 22 (June 1906): 1676.

84. Simon Flexner and James W. Jobling, "An Analysis of Four Hundred Cases of Epidemic Meningitis Treated with the Anti-Meningitis Serum," *Journal of Experimental Medicine* 10 (1908): 710.

85. Kaplan, "Dr. Flexner's Experiment," 6.

86. Kaplan.

87. Kaplan, 6.

88. Corner, *A History of the Rockefeller Institute*, 69.

89. Chernow, *Titan*, 475.

90. Chernow, 479.

91. Chernow, 676.

92. "Annual Letter 2009," Bill & Melinda Gates Foundation, accessed June 20, 2023, https://www.gatesfoundation.org/ideas/annual-letters/annual-letter-2009.

93. From inception until January 31, 2023, JSF's annual nominal return was 9.4 percent. Inflation was 2.5 percent, and JSF's real return since inception was 6.9 percent.

94. In Canada, foundations are required to distribute a minimum of 3.5 percent of the first $1 million of their endowment and 5 percent of any amount above $1 million.

95. Jeremy Siegel, *Stocks for the Long Run*, 6th ed. (New York: McGraw Hill, 2023).

96. Daniel Kahneman, *Thinking, Fast and Slow* (New York: Farrar, Straus and Giroux, 2011).

97. Carl Richards, *The Behavior Gap: Simple Ways to Stop Doing Dumb Things with Money* (New York: Portfolio, 2012), 15.

98. Warren Buffett, "2016 Letter to Investors of Berkshire Hathaway," Berkshire Hathaway, accessed June 24, 2023, https://www.berkshirehathaway.com/

letters/2016ltr.pdf. Mr. Buffett's letter is lively and instructive and at page 24 he concludes: "The bottom line: When trillions of dollars are managed by Wall Streeters charging high fees, it will usually be the managers who reap outsized profits, not the clients. Both large and small investors should stick with low-cost index funds."

99. John Bogle, *The Little Book of Common Sense Investing: The Only Way to Guarantee Your Fair Share of Stock Market Returns*, 10th ed. (New York: John Wiley & Sons, 2017).

100. Some experts would counsel us to reduce the position of our two top public equity managers and diversify. However, managers of this quality are uncommon and hard to find. They have closed their doors to new money and if we reduce our positions, we cannot later increase them. As long as these managers retain their key people and stick to their investment style, we will likely continue, regardless of short-term results.

101. Buffett, "2016 Letter to Investors," 21–23. It is worth noting that the S&P 500 index went down 37 percent in 2008 and the hedge funds substantially outperformed it in that year. Over the ten-year period, however, the index fund outperformed the hedge funds by a wide margin.

102. Mike Miller, CFA, is the former head of global equites at BMO Capital Markets and a finance lecturer at McMaster University. He is also a JSF board member. This section is based upon his continuing education talk to the JSF board, staff, and consultants on ESG in 2020.

103. "Fiduciary Duty," Principles for Strong Investing, accessed July 7, 2023, https://www.unpri.org/policy/fiduciary-duty.

104. Peter Lynch, *One Up on Wall Street: How to Use What You Already Know to Make Money in the Market* (New York: Penguin Books, 1989).

105. John Allen Paulos, *A Mathematician Plays the Stock Market* (New York: Basic Books, 2003), dedication.

106. James Collins and Jerry Porras, *Built to Last: Successful Habits of Visionary Companies* (New York: Harper Collins, 1994).

107. Richard P. Chait, William P. Ryan, and Barbara E. Taylor, *Governance as Leadership: Reframing the Work of Nonprofit Boards* (New York: John Wiley and Sons, 2005). See also Cathy Trower, *The Practitioner's Guide to Governance as Leadership: Building High-Performing Nonprofit Boards* (San Francisco: Jossey Bass, 2013).

108. In 1974, Jerry B. Harvey, professor of management science at George Washington University, outlined a common communication breakdown, which he illustrated with a story he called the "Abilene Paradox." To paraphrase, a young man, Jerry, and his wife are visiting her parents in Coleman Texas. It is a hot summer day, and they are inside playing dominos and drinking lemonade when his father-in-law suggests that they drive to Abilene and have lunch at the diner. Jerry does not want to go, but before he can answer, his wife says that she would like that. To make her happy, Jerry agrees but secretly hopes that his mother-in-law will object. She does not, however, and they pile into his father-in-law's unairconditioned car, drive fifty-three miles in the heat and the dust, eat a dreadful lunch in Abilene, and return home, hot and exhausted. To be sociable, Jerry dishonestly asks, "Wasn't that fun?" His mother-in-law disagrees and says that she didn't want to go in the first place but agreed because everyone else was so keen. Jerry expresses his true feelings for the first time, and his wife replies that she didn't want to go either and only agreed to please him. Jerry's father-in-law has the final word. He didn't want to go to Abilene but suggested it because he was worried that his daughter and Jerry might be bored. The four of them, sensible people, had done the opposite of what they had wanted to do. The full story is worth reading and sharing with your board and can be found at http://web.mit.edu/curhan/www/docs/Articles/15341_Readings/Group_Dynamics/Harvey_Abilene_Paradox.pdf.

109. Collins and Porras, *Built to Last*, especially 22–42.

110. I should note that foundations are prohibited from paying travel and meal expenses for partners or for ball games and the like for anyone. This is discussed later in this chapter.

111. Trower, *The Practitioner's Guide*, 137.

112. "Our Vision, Mission, and Core Values," BoardSource, accessed July 7, 2023, https://boardsource.org/about-boardsource/vision-mission-core-values.

113. "Our Story," Candid, accessed June 20, 2023, https://candid.org/about/our-story.

114. "About Us," Center for Effective Philanthropy, accessed June 20, 2023, https://cep.org/about/.

115. By *giant*, I mean foundations with assets of $1 billion or more.

116. By *very large*, I mean foundations with assets between $500 million and $1 billion.

117. Bolduc et al., *Foundation Strategy*.

118. Kris Deiglmeier and Amanda Greco, "Why Proven Solutions Struggle to Scale Up," *Stanford Social Innovation Review*, August 10, 2018, https://ssir.org/articles/entry/why_proven_solutions_struggle_to_scale_up.

119. Carolyn Acker and Norman Rowen, "Creating Hope, Opportunity, and Results for Disadvantaged Youth," *Canadian Journal of Career Development* 12, no. 1 (2013): 63–79 (Part 1); 12, no. 2 (2013): 63–79 (Part 2). Acker and Rowen are the founders of Pathways to Education and the story of its beginning is taken from their article. Pathways has been the subject of at least two other scholarly evaluations: Philip Oreopoulos, Robert Brown, and Adam Lavecchia, "Pathways to Education: An Integrated Approach to Helping At-Risk School Students," *Journal of Political Economy* 125, no. 4 (2017); and Adam Lavecchia, Philip Oreopoulos, and Robert Brown, "Long-Run Effects from Comprehensive Student Support: Evidence from Pathways to Education," *American Economic Review: Insights* 2, no. 2 (2020): 209–24.

120. Chernow, *Titan*, 473.

121. See Joseph P. Kalt and Johnathan B. Taylor, "American Indians on Reservations: A Databook of Socioeconomic Change between the 1990 and 2000 Censuses," Harvard Project on American Indian Economic Development, January 2005. https://www.hks.harvard.edu/publications/american-indians-reservations-databook-socioeconomic-change-between-1990-and-200; and Joseph Kalt, "Address to US Congress," March 13, 2007, https://hwpi.harvard.edu/files/hpaied/files/kalthouseapprop03-13-07.pdf.

122. Ann Christiano and Annie Neimand, "Stop Raising Awareness Already," *Stanford Social Innovation Review*, Spring 2017, https://ssir.org/articles/entry/stop_raising_awareness_already.

123. Andrea Brock and Ellie Buteau, "Grantees' Limited Engagement with Foundations' Social Media," Center for Effective Philanthropy, 2012. https://www.kaporcenter.org/wp-content/uploads/2012/08/CEP_Social-Media-Report.pdf.

124. The term *Indian Country* might seem offensive to some (particularly Canadian) readers, but it is used proudly by Indigenous Peoples in the United States. According to the National Congress of American Indians, the oldest and largest organization of tribal nations in the United States, 'Indian country' is the term for the area over which the federal government and tribal nations exercise primary jurisdiction. It is a term with a distinct meaning in legal and policy

contexts. 'Indian Country' (both words capitalized) is a broader term used to refer more generally to tribal governments, Native communities, cultures, and peoples" (National Congress of American Indians, *Tribal Nations and the United States: An Introduction*, Washington, DC: National Congress of American Indians, 2020, https://www.ncai.org/tribalnations/introduction/Indian_Country_101_Updated_February_2019.pdf, 28).

125. Meg Dunn, "This Unique Mentorship Program Helps Students with Learning Differences Realize 'Their Brains Are Beautiful,'" CNN, March 18, 2021, https://www.cnn.com/2021/03/18/us/learning-disabilities-education-dyslexia-adhd-mentorship-cnnheroes/index.html.

126. Our experience had been supporting this idea for years and in it we were strongly influenced by Robert Putnam, *Our Kids: The American Dream in Crisis* (New York: Simon and Schuster, 2016).

127. This program was originally the Florida Opportunities Scholarship (FOS). In 2014 an anonymous donor gave $10 million on condition that it be renamed the Machen Florida Opportunities Scholarship (MFOS).

128. Sarah Dewees and Benjamin Marks, *Investing for Growth: Supporting the Next Generation of American Indian Leaders* (Longmont, CO: First Nations Development Institute, 2013).

129. Daniel Stewart and Molly Pepper, "Close Encounters: Lessons from an Indigenous MBA Program," *Journal of Management Education* 35, no. 1 (2011): 66–83. https://www.doi.org/10.1177/1052562910384375.

130. Gonzaga University School of Business Administration, "U.S. News Ranks Gonzaga's MBA Programs among Nation's Best," Gonzaga University, March 29, 2022, https://www.gonzaga.edu/news-events/stories/2022/3/29/us-news-mba-2022.

131. Anand Giridharadas, *Winners Take All: The Elite Charade of Changing the World* (New York: Penguin Random House, 2018).

132. Giridharadas, 9–10.

Bibliography

Abelson, Reed, with Elisabeth Rosenthal. "Charges of Shoddy Practices Taint Gifts of Plastic Surgery." *New York Times*, November 24, 1999. https://www.nytimes.com/1999/11/24/world/charges-of-shoddy-practices-taint-gifts-of-plastic-surgery.html.

Acker, Carolyn, and Norman Rowen. "Creating Hope, Opportunity, and Results for Disadvantaged Youth." *Canadian Journal of Career Development* 12, no. 1 (2013): 63–79 (Part 1); 12, no. 2 (2013): 63–79 (Part 2).

Bill & Melinda Gates Foundation. "Annual Letter 2009." Accessed June 20, 2023. https://www.gatesfoundation.org/ideas/annual-letters/annual-letter-2009.

Bill & Melinda Gates Foundation. "Stronger, Smaller High Schools to Help Thousands of Oregon Students." Accessed June 18, 2023. https://www.gatesfoundation.org/ideas/media-center/press-releases/2003/04/oregon-small-schools-initiative.

Billings, J. S. "Cerebrospinal Meningitis in New York City during 1904 and 1905," *Journal of American Medicine* 46, no. 22 (June 1906): 1676.

BoardSource. "Our Vision, Mission, and Core Values." Accessed July 7, 2023. https://boardsource.org/about-boardsource/vision-mission-core-values.

Bogle, John. *The Little Book of Common Sense Investing: The Only Way to Guarantee Your Fair Share of Stock Market Returns.* 10th ed. New York: John Wiley & Sons, 2017.

Bolduc, Kevin, Ellie Buteau, Greg Laughlin, Ron Ragin, and Judith A. Ross. *Foundation Strategy: Beyond the Rhetoric*. Cambridge, MA: Center for Effective Philanthropy, 2007. https://cep.org/portfolio/beyond-the-rhetoric-foundation-strategy-2/.

Brock, Andrea, and Ellie Buteau. *Grantees' Limited Engagement with Foundations' Social Media*. Cambridge, MA: Center for Effective Philanthropy, 2012. https://www.kaporcenter.org/wp-content/uploads/2012/08/CEP_Social-Media-Report.pdf.

Buchanan, Phil. *Giving Done Right*. New York: PublicAffairs, 2019.

Buffett, Warren. "2017 Letter to Investors of Berkshire Hathaway." Berkshire Hathaway Inc. Accessed June 24, 2023. https://www.berkshirehathaway.com/letters/2016ltr.pdf.

Buteau, Ellie, Naomi Orensten, and Charis Loh. *The Future of Foundation Philanthropy: The CEO Perspective*. Cambridge, MA: Center for Effective Philanthropy, 2016. https://cep.org/portfolio/future-foundation-philanthropy-ceo-perspective/.

Canada Revenue Agency. "Qualified Donees." Last modified January 11, 2017. https://www.canada.ca/en/revenue-agency/services/charities-giving/charities/policies-guidance/qualified-donees.html.

Canada's Historic Places. "Carnegie's Canadian Libraries." Accessed June 16, 2023. https://www.historicplaces.ca/en/pages/34_carnegie.aspx.

Candid. "Our Story." Accessed June 20, 2023. https://candid.org/about/our-story.

Candid. "U.S. Social Sector." Accessed June 15, 2023, https://candid.org/explore-issues/us-social-sector/organizations.

Carnegie, Andrew. "The Gospel of Wealth." *North American Review* (1889).

Center for Effective Philanthropy, "About Us." Accessed June 20, 2023. https://cep.org/about/.

Chait, Richard P., William P. Ryan, and Barbara E. Taylor. *Governance as Leadership: Reframing the Work of Nonprofit Boards*. New York: John Wiley and Sons, 2005.

Chernow, Ron. *Titan: The Life of John D. Rockefeller, Sr.* New York: Random House, 1998.

Christiano, Ann, and Annie Neimand. "Stop Raising Awareness Already," *Stanford Social Innovation Review* (Spring 2017). https://ssir.org/articles/entry/stop_raising_awareness_already.

Collins, James, and Jerry Porras. *Built to Last: Successful Habits of Visionary Companies*. New York: Harper Collins, 1994.

Commonfund. *A Common Vision: Working in Partnership for the Benefit of All, 1971–1996*. Connecticut: Commonfund, 1996.

Corner, George W. *A History of the Rockefeller Institute*. New York: Rockefeller Institute Press, 1964.

Davis Investments. "Timeless Wisdom for Creating Long-Term Wealth." Accessed June 18, 2023, https://davisfunds.com/downloads/TW.pdf.

Deiglmeier, Kris, and Amanda Greco. "Why Proven Solutions Struggle to Scale Up." *Stanford Social Innovation Review* (August 2018). https://ssir.org/articles/entry/why_proven_solutions_struggle_to_scale_up.

Dewees, Sarah, and Benjamin Marks. *Investing for Growth: Supporting the Next Generation of American Indian Leaders*. Longmont, CO: First Nations Development Institute, 2013.

Dunn, Meg. "This Unique Mentorship Program Helps Students with Learning Differences Realize 'Their Brains Are Beautiful.'" CNN, March 18, 2021. https://www.cnn.com/2021/03/18/us/learning-disabilities-education-dyslexia-adhd-mentorship-cnnheroes/index.html.

Flexner, James Thomas. *An American Saga*. Boston: Little, Brown, 1984.

Flexner, Simon, and James W. Jobling. "An Analysis of Four Hundred Cases of Epidemic Meningitis Treated with the Anti-Meningitis Serum," *Journal of Experimental Medicine*, no. 10 (1908): 710.

Frumkin, Peter, *The Essence of Strategic Giving*. Chicago: University of Chicago Press, 2006.

Giridharadas, Anand. *Winners Take All: The Elite Charade of Changing the World*. New York: Penguin Random House, 2018.

Gladwell, Malcolm. *Outliers: The Story of Success*. Boston: Little, Brown, 2009.

Gonzaga University School of Business Administration. "U.S. News Ranks Gonzaga's MBA Programs among Nation's Best." Gonzaga University. March 29, 2022. https://www.gonzaga.edu/news-events/stories/2022/3/29/us-news-mba-2022.

Grant, Adam. *Think Again*. New York: Random House, 2021.

Gregorian, Vartan. "Libraries and Andrew Carnegie's Challenge," *Report of the President 1998*. New York: Carnegie Foundation, 1998.

Harper, Kenn. *Minik: The New York Eskimo*. Hanover, NH: Steerforth Press, 2017.

Internal Revenue Service. "Qualifying Distributions—In General." Last modified January 9, 2023. https://www.irs.gov/charities-non-profits/private-foundations/qualifying-distributions-in-general.

Internal Revenue Service. "SOI Tax Stats—Annual Extract of Tax-Exempt Organization Financial Data." Last modified April 4, 2013. https://www.irs.gov/statistics/soi-tax-stats-annual-extract-of-tax-exempt-organization-financial-data.

Kahneman, Daniel. *Thinking, Fast and Slow*. New York: Farrar, Straus and Giroux, 2011.

Kalt, Joseph. "Address to US Congress." March 13, 2007. https://hwpi.harvard.edu/files/hpaied/files/kalthouseapprop03-13-07.pdf.

Kalt, Joseph P., and Johnathan B. Taylor. "American Indians on Reservations: A Databook of Socioeconomic Change between the 1990 and 2000 Censuses." Harvard Project on American Indian Economic Development. January 2005. https://www.hks.harvard.edu/publications/american-indians-reservations-databook-socioeconomic-change-between-1990-and-200.

Kaplan, M. S. "Dr. Flexner's Experiment." *Rockefeller University Research Profiles*, Book 30. New York: Rockefeller University, 1987. https://digitalcommons.rockefeller.edu/research_profiles/30.

Keane, George F. "A Brief History: A Dream Fulfilled." In *A Common Vision: Working in Partnership for the Benefit of All*, 1971–1996, 20. Connecticut: Commonfund, 1996.

Lankford, Kelly Lara. "Home Only Long Enough: Arctic Explorer Robert E. Peary, American Science, Nationalism, and Philanthropy, 1886–1908." PhD diss., University of Oklahoma, 2003. https://hdl.handle.net/11244/603.

Lavecchia, Adam, Philip Oreopoulos, and Robert Brown. "Long-Run Effects from Comprehensive Student Support: Evidence from Pathways to Education," *American Economic Review: Insights* 2, no. 2 (2020): 209–24.

Lynch, Peter. *One Up on Wall Street: How to Use What You Already Know to Make Money in the Market*. New York: Penguin Books, 1989.

Nasaw, David. *Andrew Carnegie*. New York: Penguin Books, 2006.

National Congress of American Indians. *Tribal Nations and the United States: An Introduction*. Washington, DC: National Congress of American Indians, 2020. https://www.ncai.org/tribalnations/introduction/Indian_Country_101_Updated_February_2019.pdf

New Oxford American Dictionary. 3rd ed. New York: Oxford University Press, 2010.

Operation Smile. "Global Outreach." Accessed July 7, 2023. https://www.operationsmile.org/global-outreach.

Oreopoulos, Philip, Robert Brown, and Adam Lavecchia. "Pathways to Education: An Integrated Approach to Helping At-Risk School Students," *Journal of Political Economy* 125, no. 4 (2017): 947–84.

Paulos, John Allen. *A Mathematician Plays the Stock Market*. New York: Basic Books, 2003.

Petrone, Penny, ed. *Northern Voices*. Toronto: University of Toronto Press, 1988.

Philanthropic Foundations of Canada. "Canadian Foundation Facts." Accessed June 15, 2023. https://pfc.ca/canadian-foundation-facts/.

Philanthropy Roundtable. "John Rockefeller Sr." Accessed July 7, 2023. https://www.philanthropyroundtable.org/hall-of-fame/john-rockefeller-sr/.

Principles for Strong Investing. "Fiduciary Duty." Accessed July 7, 2023. https://www.unpri.org/policy/fiduciary-duty.

Putnam, Robert. *Our Kids: The American Dream in Crisis*. New York: Simon and Schuster, 2016.

Richards, Carl. *The Behavior Gap: Simple Ways to Stop Doing Dumb Things with Money*. New York: Portfolio, 2012.

Rosenthal, Elisabeth, with Reed Abelson. "Whirlwind of Facial Surgery by Foreigners Upsets China." *New York Times*, November 25, 1999. https://www.nytimes.com/1999/11/25/world/whirlwind-of-facial-surgery-by-foreigners-upsets-china.html.

Schindler, Steven. "Case 23: Preventing Crashes on America's Highways, Dorr Foundation, 1952." In *Casebook for the Foundation: A Great American Secret*, edited by Joel Fleishman, Scott Kohler, and Steven Schindler, 66–69. New York: PublicAffairs, 2007.

Schneider, Jack. "Small Schools: The Edu-Reform Failure that Wasn't." *EducationWeek* (February 2016). https://www.edweek.org/leadership/opinion-small-schools-the -edu-reform-failure-that-wasnt/2016/02.

Siegel, Jeremy. *Stocks for the Long Run*. 6th ed. New York: McGraw Hill, 2023.

Simpson, Elizabeth. "'Smile' Charity Leaders in midst of Decade-Long Feud." *Virginian-Pilot,* December 20, 2009.

Smile Train. "Donate Now and Change a Child's Life Forever." Accessed June 18, 2023. https://donate.smiletrain.org/givenow.

Smile Train. "Smile Train Audit Report 2019." Accessed June 18, 2023. https://www. smiletrain.org/sites/default/files/2021-01/smile-train-audit-report-fy19.pdf.

Somerville, Bill. *Grassroots Philanthropy: Fieldnotes from a Maverick Grantmaker*. Berkley: Heydey, 2008.

Stamberg, Susan. "How Andrew Carnegie Turned His Fortune into a Library Legacy." *NPR*, August 1, 2013. https://www.npr.org/2013/08/01/207272849/ how-andrew-carnegie-turned-his-fortune-into-a-library-legacy.

Stewart, Daniel, and Molly Pepper. "Close Encounters: Lessons from an Indigenous MBA Program," *Journal of Management Education* 35, no. 1 (2011): 66–83. https:// www.doi.org/10.1177/1052562910384375.

Trower, Cathy. *The Practitioner's Guide to Governance as Leadership: Building High-Performing Nonprofit Boards*. San Francisco: Jossey Bass, 2013.

Zinsmeister, Karl. *The Almanac of American Philanthropy*. Washington, DC: Philanthropy Roundtable, 2016.

Index

About the Author

Malcolm Macleod was appointed president and CEO of the Johnson Scholarship Foundation in 2001. During his 19-year leadership, the Foundation matured from a young family foundation to a high-quality and effective grantmaker with a private endowment of $250 million and an annual grant budget of $10 million. The Foundation makes grants in the United States and Canada, and focuses on Indigenous Peoples, the underserved, and people with disabilities. It has achieved top quartile investment returns, developed innovative grantmaking strategies, and attracted a stellar board of directors.

Born in Amherst, Nova Scotia, Malcolm obtained a Bachelor of Arts with first division honours and attended the University of New Brunswick Law School on a Beaverbrook Scholarship. He practiced law in Nova Scotia with the firm of Patterson, Smith, and its successors for 25 years. During that time, he served as chair of the firm's litigation department and as managing partner. He served as chair of the Nova Scotia Advisory Committee on Federal Judicial Appointments and was appointed Queen's Counsel in 1997.

Malcolm is board chair for the Johnson Scholarship Foundation and serves as a volunteer member of the board of the Fundy Community Foundation. Malcolm is a private consultant to grantmaking foundations in the United States and Canada.

For more details, please visit **malcolmmacleodauthor.com**